THERE IS A LAST TIME FOR EVERYTHING

A memoir of our path through Alzheimer's

PATTY GESSNER

AuthorHouse™
1663 Liberty Drive
Bloomington, IN 47403
www.authorhouse.com
Phone: 833-262-8899

Because of the dynamic nature of the Internet, any web addresses or links contained in this book may have changed
since publication and may no longer be valid. The views expressed in this work are solely those of the author and do
not necessarily reflect the views of the publisher, and the publisher hereby disclaims any responsibility for them.

Any people depicted in stock imagery provided by Getty Images are models,
and such images are being used for illustrative purposes only.
Certain stock imagery © Getty Images.

This book is printed on acid-free paper.

ISBN: 979-8-8230-2743-4 (sc)
ISBN: 979-8-8230-2744-1 (e)

Library of Congress Control Number: 2024910493

Print information available on the last page.

Published by AuthorHouse 06/13/2024

authorHOUSE®

Unable are the loved to die, for love is immortality ~ Emily Dickenson

Dedication

This memoir is dedicated to all the beautiful souls lost to Alzheimer's. May your path be paved with love, patience, mercy and the warmth that comes from knowing *you* are not forgotten.

Contents

Introduction

Odds are you know someone afflicted with Alzheimer's. But to live with someone who is progressing through the stages is when shit gets real. The title of this memoir comes from one of the lessons I learned along the way. There is a last time for everything. A last time to drive, a last time to cook, a last time to speak. Picture a path paved with stepping stones. But instead of adding stones, stones disappear one by one until there are none left and your path ends.

It took more than three years after the death of my mother to finally start writing our story. What motivated me to finally begin writing was watching close friends go through the same relentless, predictable stages with their parents and seeing the same look of defeat on their faces, hearing the same despair in their voices, and knowing the palpable heartache of watching your parent disappear piece by piece.

Although the accounts I will share are raw, my hope is that this memoir will bring comfort to other families. Comfort in knowing your emotions, your exhaustion, your experiences whether similar or different to these are real and you are not alone. Perhaps relieve a bit of the heavy guilt that creeps into your daily thoughts. Guilt of not doing enough, not sacrificing your needs enough, not being as sad as others when your loved one passes away.

I am by no means an expert on the topic of Alzheimer's. I made plenty of mistakes along the way. This memoir merely provides a perspective from a nurse practitioner, caregiver, and daughter.

This is my family's story.

(Family portrait taken in June 2015. Left to right: Claire, Mary Angela, Theresa, Eddie, Rich, Aldo, Anthony, Nara, Jim, Samantha, Sonia, me)

Chapter One: The Elusive Diagnosis

It is difficult to say exactly when Mom crossed over from normal aging forgetfulness to Alzheimer's. What started as repetitive storytelling, and forgetting where she put her keys, seemed to progress to full-blown dementia overnight. What I can remember is our family alluding to the fact Mom had a memory disorder or brushing it off as a benign consequence of aging. Somewhere between Mom not finding her keys and the start of the hallucinations, we did eventually figure it out. Yet, our family never really said the word Alzheimer's out loud until Mom was in the final stages.

Looking back, I would say Mom was in the early stages between 2012-2014. Similar to many, the formal diagnosis comes when the victim is at Stage 3 or 4. She was experiencing more anxiety than baseline and her ability to concentrate was becoming more of a challenge. Because Mom was never really asked to perform complex or new tasks, she hid symptoms well in the early stages. Once it became clear, we did everything you were supposed to do for a loved one. We started medications, sought council with specialists, and had advanced imaging. Those were also the years we felt empowered to change the course of the disease. We even looked to enroll Mom in research studies, but as it turned out, she would not be eligible. Researchers needed candidates who spoke English as a primary language and who had completed at least an 8th grade level of education. This would be our first last. The last time we would foolishly hope for a cure. While it was too late for Mom, that does not mean there won't be advancements in the future. There are research trials in progress that target prevention and early detection. There are also medications which help slow progression so there is hope for a better tomorrow.

Let me take a step back to help you understand who Nara Giuntini really was. Nara Dolina Pieroni was born on July 8th, 1937. Nara grew up in Italy during WWII with her sisters Franca and Simonetta (Simi). She, being female, was pulled out of school after completing the fifth grade. There was no need for women to continue with school because their place was to tend the home. Despite the lack of higher education, Mom was very smart, spoke two languages, was an expert seamstress, an artist, an excellent cook, a generous person, and a caring mom, aunt, grandmother and friend. She was clearly right-brain dominant, which made her well-loved.

As a child, Mom grew up on a farm in a tiny village high up in the mountains of Tuscany. Her earliest jobs at home included caring for the family cow and fetching water. She always told the story of how she almost killed the family cow. One afternoon, it was time to head back to the barn, and the stubborn heifer would not budge. Mom, frustrated, threw a rock and hit the cow in the forehead, rendering the animal unconscious. She ran home and hid in her bedroom awaiting the wrath once the murder was discovered. Mom peaked out her window and saw some of the townspeople gathering when all of the sudden, the cow woke up and stood up. Relieved, she returned to her duties. Not sure she ever admitted what she had done before her family had made the voyage across the Atlantic. Mom had an orange tabby cat named Fragolino, which means little strawberry. She absolutely adored this cat. She told us stories of how she would swaddle him and push him around in a baby stroller. She would go off and play with her friends or do chores while this cat enjoyed a nap in the stroller. The story ends badly as times were tough. The cat went missing, and Mom was told he was caught and eaten.

Growing up during WWII left lasting memories. She recalled times when she would hear bombers fly overhead and would throw herself to the ground as her father instructed, her father having to hide during the daylight hours to avoid capture by the German army, and being given chocolate candy from the American soldiers. One night, her mother heard that German soldiers were nearby. My grandmother decided it would be best to have Nara and Franca sleep in the barn with the lights out. A knock came on the door. It was the town priest who told my grandmother German soldiers were at his home and they demanded wine. My grandmother was able to provide a jug from the barrels in the barn. After the priest left, Mom complained that she felt wet. My grandmother hushed her, fearful that the Germans would be able to hear the voices of these young girls. Mom woke up the next morning to find herself in a puddle of wine. As it turned out, my grandmother did not close the spigot completely. Not your typical childhood to say the least.

(Taken 1944: Nara is pictured in front with the little white dress, to the left of her is her older sister Franca. The tall man in the back is Nara's father, and the woman with her arms folded is Nara's mom. Nara's younger sister, Simi wasn't born yet.)

(Nara at approximately 16 years old. Dad carries this picture along with a photo of their wedding in his wallet to this day.)

Nara met Aldo in 1956 when she was only 19. However, 19 was considered too old to be single in the 1950's, and she was in fear of becoming a spinster. Nara's cousin was engaged to a gentleman who knew Aldo Giuntini and thought the two of them might be a good match. Aldo was out dancing until dawn and had just fallen asleep when Mauro Cola knocked on his door. It was only 7am. He told Aldo he was to meet Nara. The men drove their motorcycles in the snow to meet Nara and her cousin. The women had to walk down the mountain from their hometown since there were no roads. The day would be spent at Aldo's aunt's home with the aunt acting as chaperone. When evening came, the snow had turned to ice and it would not be safe to drive the women on the back of the motorbikes. Aldo called upon a friend he knew to help him access a car. The two of them decided to "borrow" the car from someone they knew who was on holiday. Aldo detailed how he and his friend pushed the car out of the garage and started it when they were a safe distance away. The men drove the women back to where they were picked up, and the women walked back up the mountain to their hometown. The car was then safely returned to its garage. Dating was very simple and mostly entailed sitting at a relative's house in the company of others. After only a few dates, Aldo was ready to settle down, but Nara wanted time to think about a life together. Nara's father had already immigrated to the United States during this courtship. Nara's mother wrote to him to ask permission for the relationship. Nara's father had known Aldo's father so he gave his blessing, assuming Aldo was of the same character. Meanwhile, Aldo was growing impatient with Nara's ambivalence and decided to give her time apart to decide. After the ultimatum, Aldo had gotten into two serious accidents only weeks apart. When Nara learned of this, she decided to move forward with the relationship. While I never asked Mom directly, I would guess that she couldn't bear the thought of losing him.

(Nara and Aldo in 1956, just after they started dating)

Now engaged, Nara immigrated to the United States in 1957 with her mother and Simi, who was 7 at the time, to join her father who had settled in Illinois. The voyage was by boat on the Christopher Columbus ship and took weeks to cross the Atlantic. Nara and Simi were both extremely seasick by the time they arrived on Ellis Island, unable to keep any food down. Nara's father had arranged for someone to meet the three of them and escort them to the train to Chicago. Simi recalls feeling extremely hungry once on land, but they would have to wait until arriving at their new home for a meal. Once they arrived at their new housing provided by Nara's aunt, they were fed and settled in. I give a lot of credit to immigrants like my family. It was no easy feat to orchestrate safe passage at a time when there was no internet, limited phones, and reliance on the postal service to cross the Atlantic.

In 1958, Nara traveled back to Italy alone to marry Aldo. After the wedding, Aldo had to stay behind in Italy until his Visa was approved. Back in the 50's, this took years. Meanwhile, Nara traveled back to the US and found work at a clothing manufacturing company in downtown Chicago. She was well respected and was asked to be the manager of the men's suits division, but Mom declined given that she did not like conflict and would rather just be in the rank and file. Mom and Dad were reunited in November 1961, and just about a year later, my brother Rich was born. Nara worked at the clothing factory until she became pregnant with me, her second and last child. The company told her that she would not be able to return if she took maternity leave, so she never went back. By the year 1974, Mom and Dad became naturalized citizens.

(May 5th, 1958: Nara and Aldo's wedding. The procession towards the church was on foot from Tiglio Basso, to Tiglio Alto. Translated simply means they walked from the low parts of Tiglio to the high part where the church was located. No street existed at that time. Nara was escorted by her grandfather. Her mother, father, and younger sister could not travel back from the states to attend the wedding.)

The priest was Aldo's cousin Don Cola.
The little boy was the ring bearer, and I am
Facebook friends with his kids to this day.
The man standing, looking towards Nara, was
her brother-in-law Mauro, married to Franca.

Rich born 1962

Patty born 1968. Side note: Rich
hated taking pictures

After my birth in 1968, Nara was a homemaker. She kept a meticulously clean home. She fed us delicious meals every day. Our home was forever stocked with homemade broth, bread, sauces, preserves, pasta, prosciutto, sausage, sweets, and yes – wine and spirits. My friends and my children's friends still rave about mom's cooking. Many have asked me if I was able to memorialize Mom's recipes. The answer is, some of them. Nara didn't have a cookbook to guide her; she learned from her mother who learned from her mother and so on. I kept a few of Nara's handwritten recipes to have as a memento. Here is one for Cantuccini, which are small versions of biscotti.

Cantuccini
3 and ¼ cup flour
1 and ½ cup sugar
1 and ½ tablespoon yeast
1 stick of butter
3 eggs
Honey
Almonds

And that is all she wrote, yet they came out scrumptious and delightful every time.

However, not all meals were well received. One of my not-so-pleasant childhood memories was having to explain my lunch to schoolmates. American children (yes, I considered myself Italian throughout my childhood), could not understand why I would have blood sausage or egg yolk sandwiches instead of PB & J. That, plus being the tallest kid in kindergarten, was enough to make me wish my clothes were store-bought instead of hand-made so at least I could be less conspicuous. Still, I had it a little better than my brother. He went to kindergarten speaking only Italian at a time when teachers really couldn't tutor children who didn't speak English. Didn't matter – my brother and I both figured it out. We both attended college and have successful careers. He earned his Master's and I my Doctorate. Mom was so very proud of us. Rich and I each started our own families. Rich married Theresa and had four children, Anthony, Mary Angela, Claire and Eddie. I married Jim and together we had Sonia and Samantha.

(1999)

(2011)

Looking back, Mom led a simple life. She never learned to drive. She found work as a housekeeper for a friend after I was old enough to be in school full-time. Nara retired from housekeeping in 2005, which is the same year she and Dad moved out of the city and into a home in my neighborhood. She helped raise my children and others and loved taking care of my pets, especially our cat Sadie. She would walk my dogs and pick up the kids from school. Everything she did was a routine. Even going to the grocery store was a routine. Dad brought her once a week, and she always stocked the same items, rarely straying from the norm. My family reflects on this and believes this may have masked early symptoms. Routine equals muscle memory. The more you do the same thing, the less you have to think about the actual task, and unused areas of your brain begin to atrophy.

(Nara with all of the pets)

I do have a memory of mom showing signs in 2013 when we were visiting Rich in Colorado. By now, Mom was pretty repetitive with her stories but had no other real symptoms. Mom was behaving a little silly, but that wasn't unusual for her. My brother recalls that she was also feeling under the weather that week. We took a trip towards Mt. Evans. There is a road that takes tourists up to the summit, which is 14 thousand feet above sea level. Somewhere between 11 and 12 thousand, we stopped in a beautiful field filled with flowers. Mom became extremely disoriented. Yes, altitude was to blame. However, I recall it was a palpable, almost exaggerated response. If you recall, Mom grew up in the mountains and traveled to Italy often, so she was not new to altitude. My sister-in-law, Theresa, stayed back with Mom so the rest of us could reach the summit. Upon our return to the base of the mountain, Mom was back to baseline.

In 2014, we began noticing behavior that was out of character. We were at Mom's for dinner, and she was slamming shots of moonshine without regard. It was her attempt at being funny but was not able to process the consequences.

We had a routine that I would call her on my way home from work. This was usually between 8 and 9pm. It was a 10-minute call most nights. Enough to hear about her day. This was the year she would start repeating the same story during the call. The conversation would start with the biggest news, and then she would make small talk and then repeat the big news not knowing she had told me a few minutes earlier. As she advanced through her disease, the story seemed to be on a loop. As soon as she was finished, she began telling it again. Later on, conversations would end quickly and without substance. There came a time when Mom stopped answering the phone as she always did on the first or second ring. Dad would answer and yell for Mom to pick up. Eventually, I had to stop calling altogether. Sadly, I can't remember our last real conversation. Part of me wishes I could remember the last time; the other part is grateful that I didn't have to mourn that loss in real time.

In 2015, we decided to have professional pictures taken. Rich and I arranged for family photos, and we created an album for mom's 78th birthday. I have fond memories of this day. Everything seemed to go well, and we spent some quality time together. We planned to use this book to help Mom remember our names in the future. This strategy didn't work, but it made us feel like we were doing something useful.

(Grandkids: Mary Angela, Samantha, Anthony, Eddie, Sonia, Claire)

Nara had another talent not yet discussed. She could play piano very well. As a child in her small town of Tiglio, with a population next to nothing, there was a small church named San Giusto. The church is something to cherish. Domed ceiling with early 1900's paintings of saints. A chandelier hung above the solid marble altar. The checkered marble floor and wood benches and railings made the church seem strong yet warm and inviting. While its capacity is around 75 people, it thinks itself as big as St. Peter's in Rome. The church is rumored to have been built under the order of a woman who wanted the right to say mass. The high priest repeatedly turned her down. Finally, he offered her a chance to say mass after she built 100 churches. The woman died after completing 99 churches. San Giusto was number 99.

When Nara was a young girl, she was taught how to play the organ by the priest. She, being the only candidate available for the job, played for each mass, wedding, and funeral. The priest gave her a music book that had all the requisite songs. She kept this book with her for her entire life.

(A page from Nara's music book she used for church)

It had been several years since my parents traveled back to Italy where most of their family resides. Finally accepting the diagnosis of Alzheimer's, Dad and I both acknowledged that we would not have much more time to travel with Mom, so we decided to attempt one last trip to Italy. My aunt Simi would join us. We figured the three of us could manage Mom if things got difficult. I had one objective, and that was to have Mom play on the church organ one more time. We made plans to go in late October of 2016. In her prime, Mom would plan her trips overseas a few months ahead of time. She would collect gifts for the family, buy new clothes, pack, unpack and pack again. The suitcases would be out for a few weeks before the flight. We chose to keep our trip a secret from Mom and surprised her with the news four days before the flight. I had collected the gifts as she would have done and helped her pack because she couldn't process what the climate would be. This would be Mom's last vacation. At this point, Mom was considered to be in Stage 5 of Alzheimer's. Symptoms of memory loss become undeniable. For example, seemingly major recent events, such as a holiday or visit with a relative, may not be remembered. For someone who previously prepared delicious meals for everyone, Mom was no longer able to put together a simple meal plan, and choices became basic and repeated. During the summer of 2016, my Dad grew beans. Mom would make beans every day as the meal. Dad and I didn't want to so much as look at a bean after that summer.

Mom was no longer able to choose proper clothing to wear for the weather conditions either. Some persons with Alzheimer's disease begin to wear the same clothing day after day unless reminded to change; this was Mom. For these reasons and more, Mom was no longer able to live independently. Gratefully, Aldo was in good health and able to manage the household. We, as a family, were very fortunate that we lived close to each other. My family lived within 2 blocks from my parents, and in 2014, Simi moved in across the street. This is the only reason we were able to keep Mom at home for so long. We were a village.

Chapter Two: Italia

Our trip began on October 30th, 2016. This chapter is intended to outline our 10-day visit with all of its emotions. It was at the airport when I decided it might be a good idea to journal this trip. Not that I journal regularly, or ever really, so this was my first time. It was just what I felt I needed to do.

We had to get to concourse C at O'Hare National Airport in Chicago. To get there, the traveler needs to take a tunnel beneath the taxi-ways where they offer moving sidewalks. In typical fashion, my dad wanted to stand still on the moving sidewalk to avoid walking, and Mom wanted to run ahead. Once at the gate, my aunt and I thought it would be fun and a safe pastime to have dinner. Dad, a man who never eats after 5pm, said he would eat on the plane, which meant he wouldn't eat until approximately 8pm. Mom, of course, would do what Dad said. Waiting at the gate was just a little annoying. Simi and I took turns following Mom around. In the rare moments when Mom rested, Simi and I would try to read. We couldn't read more than a page or two at a time because Mom kept poking us, similar to how a 4-year-old would act to get attention. Mom could not sit still or be with her own thoughts – she was always in go mode. I can't remember the last time Mom could sit still to read something on her own, but I believe it was in 2014. I went so far as to get her a library card and checked out books written in Italian as an early intervention when we still thought we could change her future, but the books were left unread. Alzheimer's robs a person of concentration.

The flight proved challenging. Mom's short attention span made us laugh as much as we felt like crying. Dad sat in the row behind us and kept asking how Mom was doing. Mom kept repeating that Dad looked pale. We tried putting a movie on, but Mom stated, "I've been watching this all day." In reality, it had been 3 minutes. She decided she wanted to watch something else but had put away her headphones. A second movie was attempted, to which mom stated, "I can't hear anything." I asked, "Where are your headphones?" She replied "I don't know." Of course, these foolish statements would escape me an embarrassing number of times. Just in the time it took me to journal this, Mom had asked me four more questions. Dad couldn't figure out why his TV was set to Japanese. He was also focused on what to have for dinner. He didn't want to eat too much (a reflexive statement that has nothing to do with reality). He also wanted to make sure I picked out something for Mom to eat as well. I gave up trying to read altogether.

Mom repeatedly left her seat. While she could put her seatbelt on, she could not remember how to take it off. Seemed benign enough to let her wander. The flight was smooth, and Mom could roam without getting lost. Not exactly sure where she would go or what she would do, but when lights came on as we got close to our layover in Munich, we discovered an excess of pillows had materialized in the unoccupied seat next to us. What started as two pillows became six while we crossed over the Atlantic. Simi and I laugh about that often.

Once in Munich, Mom thought it would be fun to run ahead again, then halfway to the gate she stated, "Hey, go slow for us old people." Our wait time in Munich was about an hour, or 12 hours in Alzheimer's time. By now, Mom was exhausted and not feeling well. The rest of the day would be tough on her. We boarded the flight for Florence without incident. On the flight, we were immediately served a sandwich and wine. Italians do it right.

In Florence, we were met by our cousin Mauro (Mauretto) Santi, a very sweet gentleman who puts up with a lot. He arranged for the rental and cell phone for Dad to use. Mauretto had even programmed the phone with Dad's contacts. Having our luggage, rental, and requisite burner phone for Aldo, our pilgrimage to Fornanci Di Barga began. Our first stop was in Mauro's home town. His daughter Silvia treated us to a lovely dinner, and we were able to recharge. As soon as we sat for the meal, I saw pure joy on my parents' faces and thought to myself, this is exactly where I need to be.

From Mauro's house, it was about an hour drive to our destination. We were greeted by my cousin Gerard who helped us take in the suitcases. We had the good fortune to stay at Maria Pilati's villa. She had hosted us once before in the late 80's, but the earthquakes had taken a toll. In the years since, Maria completed renovations, and the home stands more glorious than before. Everything from the marble floor to the region-appropriate lighting to the artwork filled our stay with warmth, custom, and tradition. The bedroom where I stayed had an ornate bedroom set. The room included a dresser with a mirror, an ardmore (homes in Italy lack closets), a nightstand, and a bed. The wood was hand carved. The dresser and nightstand had a marble top. Maria bought these pieces from someone who said they were made by a carpenter from Tiglio. There was only one, my grandfather Mario. Simi and I couldn't believe it. We did try to confirm the story but did not find more details. It does make sense, though – my grandfather made furniture and coffins during the war to make money or barter for food and other supplies.

(Mauretto is Nara and Simi's cousin. He's seen holding his granddaughter)

Another cousin Luca Casci, his wife Rafaela, and two of their children stopped by around 8pm. Mom and Dad had just gone to bed. Luca went up to surprise them, and that turned out to be a bad idea. You know when you fall asleep in a new location and wake up disoriented? It usually takes a minute or two to come back to reality. Mom could not snap out of her confused state. She was convinced we were at home in Illinois and Luca had come from Italy for a visit. First lesson of the trip, let a sleeping dog lie.

Day 1: The lost purse

Maria took Simi and me to the corner café where we enjoyed our first breakfast and the best cappuccino ever. Once we finished, we picked up something to go for Mom and Dad and walked home. Rafaela was waiting at home to take me to the grocery store, and it was then I realized I left my purse at the restaurant. We immediately returned to the café where the staff had placed the purse safely behind the counter. Rafaela and I continued on to the store. The grocery store is a bit unusual. The carts are in the parking structure. You take the cart with you and return it to the corral when you unload. Cuts out the middleman. The store is on the upper level of the parking garage. There aren't elevators but rather a ramp/escalator combo that transports you and your cart. The wheels on the cart are metal, and the ramp is a magnet. Genius level achieved. The store is like our supermarkets; the only difference is that the store in Italy also carries home-grown and artisan items as well as commercial items. The unpackaged produce must be handled with plastic gloves and weighed by the customer prior to checking out. Once weighed, a label is printed for checkout. I made the mistake of putting a bunch of bananas in my cart without a bag or label. Rafaela ran to get a label, and I received the dreaded tourist glare from the cashier. In the checkout line, Rafaela got a call from Luca who asked if I had found my purse. Turns out Mom conjured up the worst possible scenario that included me being thrown in jail for not having proper identification. She was so upset that she refused to go with Dad to visit family. Neither he nor Simi could convince her to leave. I was gone for 45 minutes.

Our next stop was the cemetery. Italians love cemeteries. Every visit includes multiple cemeteries to view our deceased loved ones. People I have never met, people who died before I was born, and people not related to anyone I know. Today, I noticed that there were a limited number of last names in our region of Italy and recognized most. Then I noticed one couple had my father's name married to a name in my mother's family tree. When I asked if they could be related, dad replied "probably." He didn't seem to be at all bothered by the possibility that he may have been related to my mother before marriage. His reaction was the equivalent of my asking him to pass the salt and him saying sure. I, on the other hand, was a little more than disturbed but decided to stop asking questions. We had lunch with my cousin Daniella and her family, who took a 1000 kilometer drive to spend one day with us, a gesture I will be forever grateful for. I was able to admire her beautiful family and observe them being a family. Gerard (Daniella's brother) and his two sons also joined us. Gerard and Dad barbequed while Daniella prepared the rest of the meal. The 12 of us sat around a table meant for 6 and enjoyed the results of their labor. The visit was a treasured memory. After the meal, Gerard took me aside and told me to be strong. He said he understood what was going on with Mom. His parents are both gone, and it was easy to see that he carries the hurt around still to this day.

(Traditional family style dinner provided by Daniella wearing the solid
blue shirt and her brother Gerard wearing the gray sweater)

Day 2: Mission accomplished

We attended mass on this day being All Saints Day. The townspeople would arrive at 11:00. The priest, who was the priest that married my parents, is my father's cousin. Of course, because we are all related. Regardless, the years have not been kind to Don Cola. He was weathered and appeared to be suffering from Alzheimer's as well. When dad greeted him, Don Cola had forgotten that he was to say mass that day. Don Cola did say mass, forgot to provide a homily, and skipped a part during the consecration of the host. Fastest mass ever.

San Giusto was the church where my mother played organ every Sunday throughout her childhood. My objective for this trip was to watch her play one more time. This was no easy feat. Don Cola agreed to let us up to the balcony where the organ and giant pipes resided. There were about 9 lopsided marble steps of varying heights to climb. For added difficulty, the depth of each step was different. My mother was not athletic and had both knees replaced in the past 5 years, but that didn't stop her from trying. She managed to get to the top of the steps with time and some difficulty only to find the door to the balcony locked. It had one of those skeleton key holes. No one knew where the key was. Defeated, I helped Mom back down. The effort was evident on her face. Then, by some miracle, the altar server found the key. Mom valiantly made it up the steps a second time. The door, if it could be called that, was only 4 feet tall and 2 ½ feet wide. She stepped through, and the rest of us followed. I wonder if she thought of herself as a young girl at that moment. She walked right over to the organ and played a flawless song without hesitation. No music to read, no practice, just pure conditioning and strong muscle memory. As soon as my mother finished playing, the priest turned out the lights in a very unceremonious fashion. Thankfully, my aunt was able to video record this miraculous moment. That bastard Alzheimer's hadn't taken everything because we were able to enjoy my mother's talent in this historical setting. My aunt and I became overwhelmed with emotion understanding what it took to make this moment happen and that it would be the last.

(San Giusto looking back from the altar. The organ perched up in the balcony.)

(The organ was built into the wall. The opening to gain access to the balcony is seen on the back wall. The top of the opening was shorter than the blue trim above the organ. Nara had to climb through the opening to get to the organ.)

(Once up on the balcony, and without prompting, Nara instinctually went to the organ and immediately began playing a song.)

Following mass, we joined the Casci's for lunch. If you look up work horse in the dictionary, you will find Laura Casci (Luca's mom). She is remarkably giving. She never lets her family lift a finger. She prepared a wonderful meal for us, which included homemade pasta, two kinds of meat, stuffed zucchini flowers, roasted potatoes, and mushrooms. What a treat. For dessert, she brought out cialdoni, the Tuscan version of pizzelles. Laura positioned herself by the kitchen and always made sure our plates were full. After lunch, Mom, Laura, Simi, and I took a long walk to Colle, which was steep and unpaved. Got to hand it to Mom for making the trek. Colle is the location of their grandparents' home. It had been bought and renovated by an English family. It was certainly worth the effort to see Mom and Simi so happy.

Day 3: Laundry

If there is one thing I missed from home, it was my washer and dryer. There was a washer in the villa but no dryer. Simi and I ran the washer the night before, which seemed to take forever, so we timed the load today. It took over 100 minutes. After a great day going to one of my favorite places, St. Pellegrino, we decided to stay in and play poker. Mom used to play poker with her friends every Friday night. This ritual started before I was born and continued through the years when she would babysit my children and well beyond. While we thought it would be fun for Mom, we quickly realized she couldn't remember anything about poker. Dad, Simi and I made it work. All throughout the evening, Mom kept checking on the laundry we hung up to dry. Since there was no dryer and it was November, we couldn't hang them outside to dry quickly. Mom fixated on the wet clothes repeatedly stating, "these are never going to dry in time to go home." We kept reminding her that we still had a week before we left, yet she continued to repeat the same statement. Simi and I couldn't move her past this. Alzheimer's seems to interfere with time perception. While a healthy person has a concept of how much time has passed, someone with Alzheimer's does not. To Mom, 5 minutes might as well have been 5 hours. Another realization was that mom gave up doing laundry. She would never allow me to wash a stitch of clothing in the past; now she didn't even think about it. Being with mom 24 hours per day had given me an accurate picture of what stage of the disease she was in. The good news was that she remained in stage 5. My aunt Franca (mom's oldest sister) was stage 6. Did I mention that my maternal grandmother had dementia as well?

There are many resources that describe the stages of Alzheimer's; here is my interpretation:

Stage 1: Symptoms are largely undetectable at this stage
Stage 2: Basic forgetfulness becomes a more frequent occurrence
Stage 3: Memory loss is noticeable to most and can interrupt daily tasks
Stage 4: Difficulties extend past memory and into more complex tasks

Stage 5: Basic tasks are more difficult, can have delusions, paranoia, and hallucinations
Stage 6: Worsening behavioral changes and decreased ability to communicate verbally
Stage 7: Physically, the person will lose the ability to walk, talk, and swallow

Some resources subdivide stage 7, but it remains the last stage.

Day 4: Anger

The day started out the same. Mom asked where her keys were and stated the laundry will never dry, yet Simi and I had completed 4 loads. We headed to breakfast, Dad said he wanted something light, and Mom said she wasn't hungry, yet they both ate. We headed out to the market before meeting up with the Casci's again. After another delicious meal, I stood up to stretch, and Mom joined me thinking it was time to leave. Maybe a trip to the restroom would do us both some good. When we returned to the table, Mom saw Laura who had been with us for the entire meal and stated, "Look who joined us for lunch?" I came to the conclusion that drinking wine with her meal was probably not a good thing for Mom any longer.

Afterwards, Simi and I spent time with Luca and his son Marco. They brought us to their town. Verni is such a small town that the birth rate is roughly 1 child every 4 to 5 years. The town is situated on top of a hill. Parking for the town is at the base, and you have to walk up the steep paths. All I kept thinking about was lugging my groceries up every week. Luca had remodeled his home beautifully. He had the most amazing view of Monte Pania.

When we returned, Mom had been fixated on why we were gone so long. She repeatedly asked about us. Went on and on. I had talked to Laura about helping Dad with Mom when Simi and I enjoyed a few days in Venice, and now she understood. She graciously agreed. She was explaining to Dad what he should do Sunday, but he kept starting new conversations. We had to scold him in order to get his attention.

Simi and I went back to Fornaci to get a few things, and again, Mom asked what took so long. That evening, I told Mom she should go shower and wash her hair. Simi and I realized Mom hadn't showered since we arrived so we thought we should gently suggest it. She said she would do it in the morning. I said fine but that I would shower first. In an effort to push the issue, I thought I could guilt her into doing it tonight. It worked. She showered. She wasn't going to wash her hair because there wasn't a hair dryer. I showed her where it was, and Dad plugged it in. She came down after finishing, looked at me, and said, "You don't have to tell me when to wash myself, I do that myself." She turned her back and went upstairs to bed upset. Dad went upstairs to go to bed and tried to talk to her. That was a mistake. She yelled at him, and then he came back down. I suggested he not talk to her tonight, just go to bed. Simi and I talked. She noticed how odd it was that Mom couldn't be apart from us in Italy because at home we had our separate lives and we were not with her 24 hours a day. Yet now, she was incessantly worried about where we were if one of us was missing. Simi was right. I didn't understand either. I thought maybe it was the result of travel, the change in environment, time zone and diet and people.

This is the kind of behavior I was expecting. I didn't know exactly how it would manifest, but I knew it would come out. I spoke with Dad while Mom was drying her hair. I said he needed to assume more of a father role and stop giving Mom choices. For example, I asked him if he knew if she was brushing her teeth. He said he tells her to brush everyday. I said, "Do you think she remembers to do it when she is in the bathroom?" He acknowledged the point. We agreed not to give her any more red wine and instructed him to use Liana and Laura to help with Mom while we were gone. I reinforced how he should not let Mom control his actions like she did when she thought I lost my purse. I wanted to make sure he got to visit as many people as he could. He somehow interpreted this as me asking him not to disturb Simi and me for the weekend. Of course, I corrected him. Aldo didn't have Alzheimer's; he had selective hearing and interpretation.

Day 5: Gone is the caregiver

Mom woke still upset, but Simi and I weren't sure if she remembered why. We weren't going to remind her. By 10 am, she was back to normal. We were going to spend the day with Liana in Barga, but it was raining and miserable out. 100% rain forecasted for the next 24 hours. We enjoyed a nice time with Liana and her kids. Liana is my dad's youngest sister who has two children (David and Francesca). I missed my cousins so and wished they were closer to me. David has two kids Matia (9) and Giorgio (6). Matia is very friendly and outgoing whereas Giorgio is more shy. Francesca and her husband Gianluca are so very sweet. She, Danielle and I spent a lot of time together when we were growing up. Francesca had not been able to have kids. They had tried everything and had also failed achieving a child through adoption. She and Gianluca were going to give it one more try. They were ultimately successful and gave birth to a beautiful baby girl. Bianca was born in January of 2018.

Dad sat at the end of the table with David and Gianluca. Mom was at the other end and upset that Dad didn't sit next to her. Of course, we didn't care where she sat, but she refused to move and refused to let Dad sit next to her. And again, she was mad that Dad wasn't next to her. She got downright mean about it. She actually started to swear at Dad across the long table, so I asked her not to speak that way. She shot me a glare that could have struck me dead on the spot. Perhaps a sign of things to come. By the time lunch was over, I was miserable with cold symptoms and wanted nothing more than to lay down. Zio Andrea (Liana's husband) had a medical issue the night before and couldn't join us for lunch. Zia invited us to visit with her at home with Andrea. Mom said no of course, which gave me an out to go home and relax. Dad wasn't going to go, but I insisted. I was finally able to convince him to go, and he dropped Simi and me off at the house. To my surprise, Mom decided to go with. She was calm and pleasant. The demon had left her.

In times past, if anyone would have sneezed or was sick in any way, Mom would dote on us until she was satisfied that we were well. Now that I was coughing, sneezing, stuffy and body aching, she was oblivious. I mourned the times Mom would care for me and others while we were ill. Being a caregiver was what she was raised to do, but those days were over. I wondered what went on her head now. Where did she go? What occupied her thoughts? Most of the time, she was stuck in a loop. Today, it was back and forth between the laundry that will never dry and that it wouldn't stop raining.

Day 6: Venice

Rafaela and Grazia (Rafaela's middle child) took us to Venice. They picked us up at 5:00 am and drove us to Lucca, where we left the car and picked up a train to Florence. There, we transferred trains and boarded for Venice. As soon as we boarded the first train, Simi and I fell asleep. Both of us would later question why this couldn't happen on an airplane.

Rafaela thought of everything. She arranged our trip and planned ahead to bring snacks on board. Such good people. I'm so grateful for them. Mom and Dad spent the day with Laura and Enzo in Tiglio. It was rainy and perfect for them to stay inside.

What a day. We arrived and left our backpacks at the hotel, then began our tour of Venice. We also found a lot of standing water. The city workers place boardwalks so that people can keep their feet dry. In some places, it can get several inches deep, and the vendors stand ready to sell you galoshes.

What a magical city. The minute you hit piazza San Marco, you can't help but be left in awe. The sheer size is overwhelming. To think it was all built by hand on water. Our first stop was Murano. There, we watched a person blow glass and make a clear vase. We were so amazed at how casually he handled the pipe and how quickly he made the shape. All of us commented on how it would have taken us years to make the most basic shape. Next, he made a horse with colored glass. He took this blob of scorching hot powder and spun it into an oblong ball, then used long-nose tweezers to pull out first its ears, then nose, then neck, then mane, then legs. All the while turning the piece and taking advantage of each angle to improve the shape and detail. A true talent indeed. After our tour of the factory, we took a stroll on the island and grabbed a quick snack. We then returned to the main island and made our way into palazzo Ducale.

This enormous structure housed the "senate" so to speak. Laws were made and sentences were carried out here. We admired the detail of the paintings and wood carvings in awe of the mosaic marble flooring. Really a sight to behold. One of my favorite spots in this building is Il Ponte di Sospiri. Once a criminal was sentenced, they would be led over this bridge. It would be the last time they would see daylight. The bridge got its name from the sighs that could be heard coming from the bridge. The prison followed. We noted the small entryways and massive iron windows to the hallway. The key hole on these doors was about 6" tall. Would have loved to see the key that opened those locks. I reflected on the fact that I was walking where all the condemned once walked centuries ago.

Once we finished in the museum, it was just about sunset. Rafaela hurried us to the piers to catch a glimpse of one of the most stunning sunsets I have ever seen. The other structures like San Giorgio and San Pietro churches were in the shadows and acted as cutout design backdrops. The whole scene was surreal. Pictures can't do it justice, but I did get a few winners for show and tell. Once satisfied that we had drunk up every minute of the sunset possible, we made our way to Ponte Rialto. This is a beautiful bridge that houses many little shops. Similar to what I have seen in Florence. We climbed up and down all the steps then back over again. Simi and I got in a little more shopping. From there, we made our way back to the hotel to clean up for dinner. The hotel was centrally located and very reasonably priced, but it had one down side. 66 steps to get to the room. Not terrible, but for Simi, who was in need of a hip replacement, it was pure hell.

We found our way back to Rialto for dinner along the waterway with the marvelous bridge as a backdrop. Simi and I had pizza for the first time this trip. She and I also finished a bottle of wine. After dinner, we shopped some more and went back to piazza San Marco for a stroll and gelato. I had rum raisin and tiramisu. Finally, the gelato that I remembered. I was hesitant to say that gelato was still as good as I remembered but now, I was sure of it. The piazza at night was lit up with both lights and life. There was live music playing, people visiting, vendors selling goods. The most romantic scene I have ever witnessed. Highly recommended. Soon after, we made our way back to the hotel to turn in for the night. I felt bad for Simi as she had to tackle 66 steps for a second time. The next morning, we walked around again until we had to catch our train back to Fornaci.

Day 8: The goodbyes start

Today was just a catch-up day. Simi and I picked up some delicious baked goods for dinner and guests that night. Oh, the smell of fresh bread! We got back to the house where Dad was waiting for us. Dad was to drop us off in Barga so we could shop while he made the last of his cemetery rounds. The plan was for Mom to come with Simi and me and give Dad a break. When we got to the drop off, mom refused to go with us and insisted on staying with Dad. I remember the look of defeat and irritation on Dad's face. Who could blame him? Mom would certainly derail his plans.

Simi and I hit some shops and then went up to the duomo of Barga. All towns have a duomo. Barga's is well known because it is set on a picturesque hilltop and is the subject of many pieces of art. Once at the top, we had a 360-degree view of the best of Tuscany. I could not stop taking pictures. I have over 800 for this trip. I had never taken that many pictures.

Simi and I made our way back to the meeting place and ordered a panino for lunch. The difference between Italian sandwiches and ones you find in America is not only the taste but the size. In Italy, you get a small roll with 2 pieces of cold cuts and maybe a slice of cheese. Sometimes arugula. Very little goes on the sandwich. Compare that to an American sub. Dad marched in at 1:30, just as we sat down to eat. He first told us about his lunch and how it was the best thing ever. Then he told us how Mom would not stop asking where we were. I asked where Mom was, and he replied, "In the car." He said she wouldn't come inside the café so he decided to go wait with her. Of course, Mom then came inside to see us, and Dad had to tell us about his lunch again.

Our next stop was to say goodbye to Tiglio. Always hard. Laura was as gracious as ever. She told me all about how she kept mom busy while we were away in Venice. It was getting late and we still had things to do, but I couldn't bring myself to suggest we leave. Finally, Massimo started us off. Simi was the first to cry, then Dad, then me. Mom didn't cry. Instead, she was acting child-like. We got out to the parking lot where I took a picture of Mom and Dad by a mini shrine of sorts. Then I heard Simi say, "Hey, I can get Pandora." What does she play? The Beatles "In My Life." I cried more. The ride back was quiet.

(Mom and dad at the mini shrine)

We stopped in Fornaci for our last gelato. I had nocciola and ciccolato con pana. Yummy, but the rum raisin was still my favorite. I had Dad drop us off in town for last-minute shopping. Again, Mom wanted to stay with Dad. Simi and I walked back to the house and ran into David, who was looking for our house. He came to say goodbye. Next came Luca and Marco and finally Rafaela. Luca kept things light, and Dad wasn't upset when they left.

Once the guests left, we had to pack. Sad for Mom. She wanted to help but no one wanted to risk losing an item or packing incorrectly, so she went to bed first.

There I was lying awake in bed on the second to last night. Thankful for the experience. Thankful for the time with family. Thankful for my parents having this last hurrah as a couple. My Dad was able to make another trip to Italy in 2022, at the age of 90, with my daughter Samantha as a travel companion.

Day 9: Last day

Every visit, dad makes sure he stops at the local paper, Giornale di Barga, to have his name included in the next edition. Here is how it works in Italy. We walked in off the street, where the editor sat at one desk and a lady at another. My dad knew the editor, of course, and of course the editor had a relationship with one of my cousins. We left our name and hometown scribbled on a piece of note paper. He said, "tutto a posto." We shook hands and left. No forms, no wait times, no cost, no fuss and sure enough, our trip was memorialized in the paper's next edition.

Dad always talked about La Pascoli. I never really understood what it meant but now I know. It's a posto riposo (retirement home) for locals. Not-for-profit organization, La Giovanna Pascoli, is a group of people back home, of which Aldo was an original board member, that serve as a committee responsible for voting in the administrators and ensuring quality care remains top priority. The retirement home used to house 125 tenants. The government stepped in and said they needed to regulate the food and residents. At that point, the committee handed over the day to day to a company out of Milano. Our committee, of which my brother and I are now members, eventually put the ownership back in hands of the people of Barga. Now the home is for profit with government subsidies and can provide service for 70 residents.

Zio Andrea was feeling better by now, and we decided to take a drive to Renaio. It was such a pretty drive. I put Mom and Dad in the car with Zio. My aunts and I enjoyed a more normal drive. Fun fact: Renaio is home to the oldest chestnut tree.

(We gathered around the old chestnut tree, affectionately known as Castagno di Annibale. The girth is a whopping 24 feet and stands 33 feet tall. The tree is estimated to be over 500 years old, some rumors have it at 720 and still produces chestnuts. Aldo is standing next to my uncle Andrea and my aunt Liana – Aldo's youngest sister – is next to Simi.)

We traveled back to Barga where we had to say our goodbyes to Liana and Andrea. Dad couldn't. Just told her he would be back for lunch next week instead. It's tough to be an 84-year-old man and not think it will be the last time you get to hold your sister. I took a picture of Liana and Andrea as we headed to the car to leave. Liana had a deep sadness on her face and was looking down. She was being held by my uncle. I thought to myself, how sad. She is going to miss her brother so much. We came to find out when we were back in America that Andrea's illness was actually advanced stage cancer. He died a few short months after our visit. My aunt's painful expression was for many reasons.

(Liana and Andrea)

We visited our cousin Loredonna at Pedona where Franca's house was. It was a tiny little town next to a paper factory. The most familiar place to me thus far. I remember walking to and from Fornaci as a little kid. I remember the trees. The smells. The sounds. The feelings as we drove past Le Case Operaie, which provides low-income housing and where my father grew up. We stayed there when I was 6 and 14 years old. I remember going to the potso, which translates to "the puddle" and is where the ladies do laundry with soap in cement tubs filled with water. This was done outside. Clothing was all hung outside to dry. If it rained, the clothes were left out another day to dry.

Alessandro, Loredonna's son, is a distant cousin and one I spent a lot of time together with one summer. We were inseparable actually. He came to visit that last night with his wife and two kids. His daughter was 18 and son 14 at the time. We shared memories and laughed at Mom trying to convince Dad to get her a cat. We spoke a lot about Aunt Franca. Alessandro knew her well. It was always hard to talk about Franca with Mom around for obvious reasons. As I mentioned before, Franca was one stage ahead of Mom. She was unable to recognize family any more, and she had memories of family but couldn't point to them even if they were standing in front of her.

Day 10: Going home

In typical fashion on the day of departure, we all awoke early and were ready by 8 am instead of 9 like we had planned. We wanted to grab one last cappuccino at our favorite cafe. Dad was too nervous that he wouldn't poop so he didn't want to go. Mom kept trying to help but everyone was afraid she would lose something that we needed. She tried helping with the garbage but didn't know what went in which container. She didn't even think of cleaning anything, which was really odd. It made me think she had regressed. I can never remember a time when my mom didn't clean. For some unknown reason, Mom was mad at Dad. It was likely she had seconds of lucidity in which she felt useless and lashed out at Dad. Simi and I told Mom to come join us and she said no because Dad wasn't going. She turned face and went upstairs, announcing that she was going back to bed fully clothed with her winter coat on. Simi and I left, which was therapeutic for me. I was able to let off some steam.

We returned from breakfast, and Dad had to tell me that Mom took her meds without eating. My dad is obsessed with a lot of things. Medicine is one of them. He is also obsessed with his bowel habits and feels the need to discuss them with our friends and family in Italy.

Now it was 8:15 and I told dad that we should relax for 45 minutes. Nope. He called Maria to come pick up the keys, which meant that we had to leave. He won. We barely fit in the car with all our bags. My poor aunt was the most squashed. I could only see 3/4 of her face from where I was sitting.

The drive back to the airport turned out to be a dangerous undertaking with Dad at the wheel. I was literally counting down the kilometers to when we would arrive at the airport. 71 km to go. My dad was having such trouble. At one point, he nearly stopped in the middle of the road to ask which way to go. 55 more km.

I programmed the navigation system in the car to get us to the airport. I told him to follow the blue line. He chose to follow the directional arrow that indicated the next turn in x number of kilometers. 43 km to go.

To know my dad is to know a man who is very fearful of bad things happening while driving. Not only is he convinced he will blow a tire, he keeps a machete in his car in the event he is attacked by wild animals. For the record, he also keeps one strapped to his bicycle. We live in a suburb of Chicago. Not quite the jungle. The other thing he fixates on is running out of gas. At home, he never lets the car go below half a tank. Again, we live in a suburb with gas stations every mile or two that are open from morning until night. Needless to say, Dad started talking about getting gas before we left the house that morning. At this point in our journey, he had mentioned getting gas about 25 times. Around the 26 km mark prior to arriving, the GPS indicated a nearby gas station. I informed Dad that he would need to get off the highway. He didn't believe me and thought there would be a station overpass similar to how it is at home on the 90. He slowed the car and hesitated to get off the highway. Let me repeat, highway. That's right, a road upon which cars travel at high speeds and no one expects a car to stop. 25 km to go. We had to stop and pay the toll upon exiting the highway. My dad said, "I don't see a gas station." I said, "We are still on the ramp." He didn't believe me and had to ask the attendant.

We went to a gas station, and the attendant asked for a "banko" card for payment so my dad asked for my credit card. The attendant had to send us away. Evidently, we didn't have the correct card for payment. 24 km.

We stopped at a second gas station, and he immediately asked an attendant if we could pay with cash. Then my dad wanted to move the car to a full serve station. I had to remind him that we were capable of figuring out how to pump gas. All that fuss and the car only needed 1 liter to top it off. Thank God we didn't run out of gas. 23 more kilometers.

The GPS then took us to the airport. There was, shall we say, a fundamental lack of signage. We could see the airport, but no signs. The first and only sign showed up at the intersection, more accurately, after the turn. You needed to be in the right lane, but we were in the middle. 5 additional km to go. This was punishment for me mumbling disrespectful things about my dad's driving. Missing the turn led us directly back onto a highway, and it did not appear to have a quick turnaround point. I re-programmed the nav system and pointed out the route to Dad. He said, "Look, the GPS remembered where we wanted to go." I pointed out that I had reset it after the 4th time he repeated himself. We made it to the airport and dropped off Mom and Simi and the luggage.

Thank God for the GPS. Even though the rental companies were only 1 kilometer away, we would never have found it. Dad didn't listen when I told him where to enter, so we went to the desk and the staff told him to go where I had said. Once parked, I grabbed the attendant so I could start the process. He had checked off the paperwork, and my dad still hadn't brought over the keys. After a quick check the attendant said we were free to go. Dad struck up a conversation and asked where to find the bus. The return lot was not big. There was only one building and in front of it was one sign that said shuttle. I said, "This way, Dad." Not good enough. He asked the attendant. I started walking, and he was still talking. I saw the shuttle and yelled to him to get moving. We made it on the shuttle.

At the airport, I struggled with getting our tickets, and Simi ended up having to check an additional bag. We got our documents and got through security. Before entering, I asked about getting a stamp for my tax-free forms. The attendant responded that it would be after security. Watching an old couple and one with Alzheimer's go through security was actually comical. My dad wouldn't listen and had to keep going back though. Mom just looked confused and needed to be led around. Her shoes didn't come through right away so she started looking for them. Talk about out of sight out of mind. We got to the gate, and there was no counter for our tax-free stamp. Dad and I would have to go back through. We left the house at 8:30 am for an airport that was about 120 km away. Boarding time was at 12:45. It was now 12:15. We went back to the security checkpoint, and I asked if we could go back for the stamp. They said yes. We were directed to the white counter. It was about 50 meters in front of us. Halfway there, Dad asked if it was here. Nope, keep walking, Dad. We got to the counter with no one else in line, small miracle. The woman could not have worked any slower to stamp our form. From there, we had to get to the next window for the refund. Done, but not quite. Dad started talking to a guy behind the glass. I had to tell him to get a move on. We got back to security, and my dad was convinced we could just sneak through without being scanned. I said I doubt it. He did his best to get the girl's attention, but they did not let him through until he was scanned again. Once through, dad stopped to talk to the security personnel again and reported to me that they were required to check us every time. Really? Imagine that. We got back to the gate with 10 minutes to spare.

Munich was interesting. We landed on time and had 45 minutes to get to the gate. In that time, we had to travel up and down 4 sets of escalators, take a shuttle, go through border patrol and show our passports and boarding passes 3 more times. Dad couldn't find his boarding pass at border control. That was fun. I didn't understand why he would put that away each and every time.

Despite the arduous journey from the Florence plane to the Munich gate, we managed to arrive with 15 minutes to spare. Once in line to board, Dad started talking to a stranger. I asked him to pay attention to how we scan our boarding pass so he knew what to do. He didn't. And he and Mom were separated. So Dad scanned his pass but didn't walk through. Mom scanned hers and then walked through Dad's gate. This sent the staff into a bit of a tailspin. Simi and I enjoyed the comic relief. We boarded and made our way to our seats.

It was a long journey, but I am so thankful that we were able to make this happen for Mom and Dad. Even if Mom didn't really understand. I like to think she felt it in her heart.

The year before the storm

The year 2017 was the last year of Mom's full independence. It was the year Mom turned 80, which we celebrated with a simple but perfect party. Later that year, Mom watched as her oldest granddaughter got married. We planned to utilize Mom's sewing talents one last time and surprise my daughter Sonia with a custom bouquet wrap. We gathered items from both families. From Keith, we collected ruffles from his great-great grandmother Mary. Rose patches came from his great grandmother Harriet. Lace trim from his grandmother Betty. His mom, Maribel, supplied pearl pins to secure the wrap to the bouquet. The base linen was hand made by Sonia's great-great grandmother Armita. The lace on the bottom was crocheted by her great grandmother Giannina. Mom embroidered a flower design and their initials on the front. Lastly, we added pearls from my wedding dress. Together, Mom and I worked on designing the wrap, and she sewed all the pieces together. The surprise was beloved and now the wrap is stored in a shadow box as the precious keepsake that it is. It would be the last time she would use her sewing machine.

(Bouquet wrap)

(Sonia and Keith's wedding September 2017. Mom held up beautifully)

Chapter Three: New Challenges

Getting lost

We have all heard stories of people with Alzheimer's getting lost. A close friend of mine lost an aunt and uncle when they got lost driving and succumbed to the elements. Our story picks up in April 2018. Mom was an avid walker. She could walk for miles and not be phased. As I stated previously, she used to pick up my dogs and walk them while I was working. She and I walked a million miles together, it was one of our favorite things to do. On April 28th, 2018, Mom got lost. Dad let her take a walk by herself. He thought it was still okay given how many times she had done so in the past. After all, she took the same route and always returned. After an hour, he became concerned and began to look for her. He drove around the neighborhood for hours, four to be exact, before he called me. I was at work and felt helpless. He hadn't thought to call sooner or notify the police. I immediately called my husband, Jim, who was home, and told him to call the police and meet at my dad's house. Simi was also home, and she joined the search. The police put out the alert so the neighboring towns would be on the lookout. Mom had left the house around 1 pm with a light windbreaker, and it being April, the afternoon turned cold. It wasn't long after we got the police involved when she was found. She had walked from home to the next suburb and wandered into a Starbucks 6 miles away. Staff could see she was disoriented and called police. I had planned to leave work but had a few patients to tend to in my ICU. Before I could finish, the ER physician called me to say, "Your mom is here." An ambulance brought her to my hospital to get checked out. She was physically fine, but mentally shaken. I remember being so angry with my father for waiting so long to call. As we packed up to take her home, she had a bowel movement on the gurney. In an attempt to save her embarrassment, Dad and I grabbed a pad and took her home where she was able to clean up and warm up. That was her last independent walk. That night, on the 10 o'clock news, another victim of Alzheimer's was lost in the city. His family desperate, there would be no rest for them.

The very next day, I took Mom to the police station so that they could have all her information on file in the event she got lost again. She couldn't understand why we were at the station because she had forgotten the entire event. Fortunately, our family was successful at preventing mom from getting lost again. In an effort to preserve some of her perceived independence, Dad and I decided we would still allow her to walk from home to my house and back. Once she left, I watched until she got to the corner, at which point I would call Dad to take over the surveillance and vice versa. We did this for her as much as we did it for our sanity. She would walk back and forth often. In fact, my neighbor has a picture of mom walking from my home to hers. He was looking at his house from the live Google Maps view, and there she was. We laughed because it was so predictable. She was always walking.

Incontinence

Incontinence is common in the middle to late stages of Alzheimer's. It is believed to be the result of several factors including the inability to process the need to eliminate. We did what we could to get mom to use the restroom before leaving the house or watching for signs. We tried to stick to stores that had easily accessible restrooms. I remember a day when I took mom to a craft store for yarn. She told me she had to use the restroom. We found it easily enough and that was that. When she came out, it was obvious that she had soiled herself yet she told me she had used the bathroom. I made up an excuse and took her home. The smell in the car was so bad, but she didn't notice. I dropped her off at home and when she got up from the car seat, she noticed the stain. She then realized what had happened and looked so upset. My heart broke for her. How humiliating. These incontinent events happened with increased frequency after that. Trips to the store became shorter and shorter. We timed any excursion after her daily bowel movement so she could save face. People would ask if we tried incontinent briefs. We did buy them, but mom wouldn't wear them. I think pride stopped her.

Meanwhile I had to deal with my emotions while cleaning up human feces from the passenger seat. No one prepares you for the anger and deep sadness that happens simultaneously. Once these emotions left, I was left with guilt that I put her in the situation, that I was angry, that I was embarrassed.

Scotch tape

Victims of Alzheimer's can exhibit repetitive behaviors. Mom went through several of these. None of us understood it or had any idea what, if anything, there was to do about it. We didn't see any harm in the activities she chose, so we let her do whatever it was. The first was an obsession with Scotch tape. She put Scotch tape on everything. Here is an example. Dad and I realized that Mom had not kept up with expirations on homemade sauces and vegetables from their garden that she kept in the freezer. One day, while I was in the freezer looking for old items to dispose of, I found some old tomato sauce. The sauce was in one of those hard plastic pencil cases kids used for school, and it was wrapped in scotch tape. I remember thinking, this person is not my mom. She would tape loose pictures to the wall and even take pictures out of their frames to tape them up instead. She used it as if it was string to hold things together. My daughter recalled that Mom taped little butterfly window decorations all over the home. It was odd and only lasted a month or two.

By now, I would be taking Mom to all of her appointments. It always amazed me how the public really has no idea how to handle patients diagnosed with Alzheimer's or dementia because the person can seem completely normal during a 15-minute visit. Staff would provide Mom with directions as if she understood what was said, or that she would remember what was said in order to follow through. Always made me chuckle when she would ask to go to the bathroom and the staff would give directions and Mom would nod a reflexive nod. A response based on the emotion and inflection provided by the speaker. I guess they would have no way of knowing they are explaining medications to a woman who stored tomato sauce in a pencil case wrapped in tape. It would be nice if Alzheimer's patients walked around with a sign that said "no really, I don't get it."

Scarves

The next big obsession was mom's knitting. She would knit day and night and made what felt like a million scarves. I will never know exactly how many because she would give them out to family and friends. If you came over for a visit, you got coffee and a scarf. Dad would get so frustrated because mom would constantly run out of yarn and he would have to take her for more. He begged me to get her to stop, but I didn't see the harm. Not to mention, my insistence would mean nothing to Mom. My dad couldn't understand this. He felt she had control over these obsessions. He also believed it wasn't good for her to fixate. Understanding the disease was not my dad's strong suit.

My parents' 60th wedding anniversary was coming up, and we planned a great celebration that also served as a family reunion. We wanted to give everyone an opportunity to remember mom in a better light than what was to come. We came up with the idea to give the scarves away as party favors. We couldn't think of a better way to put all of that hard work to good use. Many who attended tell me they still have their scarf. It warms my heart to know that Mom's memory lives on. Mom made over 60 scarves just for the party.

(The scarves were placed on display at the anniversary party for guests to choose and take home. Nara's granddaughter Claire hand-wrote the message on the chalkboard.)

The party was on July 15th, 2018 about a week after Mom's 81st birthday. Reflecting on the amount of work this party took, it was equivalent to a small wedding. We booked the venue and photographer, had invitations made, catered the meal, and had a makeshift open bar. I worked with a local bakery to re-create a cake that looked like the one from my parents' wedding. I even found a cake topper that could pass as the same one they had in 1958. In fact, 1958 is the year stamped on the bottom of the statue. Dad keeps that statue in his curio cabinet at home now. Jim made the 4-tiered cake stand, and I shopped at local antique stores for the doilies that would be placed under each cake round.

(1958 compared to 2018)

Rich let me borrow his kids to help with the decorations, and he and his wife Theresa were responsible for getting Mom and Dad to the party. My son-in-law, Keith, plays piano very well, and as luck would have it, there was a piano available at the venue. He played Elvis' "Can't Help Falling in Love" while my parents danced seemingly in their own world. The party couldn't have gone better.

(Mom and dad dancing at the anniversary party)

After we got home, Mom was out of sorts. She kept pacing back and forth from kitchen to bedroom, lost. On one return to the kitchen, she noticed the flowers we brought home from the party and asked why we had them. We reminded her they were from the anniversary party, to which she replied, "Oh no! Did I miss the party?"

No Mom, you were the life of the party.

Inappropriate behavior

There are many behaviors that become exaggerated or inappropriate as a person progresses through Alzheimer's. At least, that was our experience. Take for example physical contact. While it would be completely appropriate for adult siblings to act silly with one another, it's another to touch or grab another person inappropriately. Much less so in a public area. We attended a dinner at Aldo's Italian club in February of 2018. Mom was sitting next to Simi in a banquet hall with about 150 other club members. Mom began grabbing Simi's chest. While we laughed about it, I recall Simi crossing her arms to protect herself. Mom also started intentionally knocking over glasses at the table and laughing as if she were a toddler. Dad was so embarrassed. It was as if Mom no longer had control of her actions that would have been inhibited in the past.

Another example is related to cooking. As previously explained, my mother was an excellent cook. As her disease progressed, she retreated from complex meals altogether and fell into a routine of simple dishes. However, we did contribute to this regression because we discovered some dangerous behaviors. The last time she made spaghetti sauce, I noticed she was sampling the meat while it was raw. Historically, she would sample the sauce at a much later stage to adjust seasonings. In her mind, she was following her old routine but did not understand that the meat was raw. Another example was the day Mom cooked something that got both of them ill. Dad called me over, and boy, were they a mess. Both pale and dehydrated from repeated trips to the bathroom. We never figured out what ingredient was added that essentially caused them to have a bout of food poisoning, but it didn't matter. Dad assumed the responsibility of cooking in 2018. It took a few months, but he eventually learned some new things to cook and did such a good job providing a variety of nutritious meals, keeping the pantry stocked with their favorites. Simi and I would contribute meals as well. I remember Mom being proud of Dad and complementing the meal every time I was present. The mom I knew growing up never allowed Dad to cook because she would have viewed it as a failure of her abilities. At least Alzheimer's sheltered Mom from feeling the emotion of failure.

My parent's house was always the envy of anyone who visited for its cleanliness. Mom would mop the floors every day. We wouldn't dare walk beyond the foyer with our shoes on. Mom and Dad had this preoccupation with shoes in general. Shoes worn outside will never be worn inside. Slippers would be worn on any surface that is not carpeted. Carpeted flooring was the only place my parents would walk around in socks or bare feet. Dad has since moved into a condo where the only laminate flooring is in his 10x10 kitchen. He still wears slippers only in the kitchen and takes them off to walk around the rest of the condo. Even at this later stage, Mom would still attempt to clean, but it was infrequent. That is, unless it became a routine. She started cleaning the floors again, but Dad couldn't figure out what she was using. The floors became very slippery. So much so that I was worried one of them might fall. We also noticed that Mom would sometimes attempt to use the dishwasher but then we caught her cutting open the pods. Dad and I put the cleaning supplies where Mom could no longer get to them, and so ended Mom's cleaning.

Mom kept an old phone book with her contacts. The kind you hand wrote in. Mom started calling contacts she knew a long time ago, which was fine, but she continued to call them daily. She would thumb through the book and call every day. At first, Dad and I would erase some of the contacts, but we ultimately had to "lose" the phone book for everyone's sanity.

Jim, Samantha and I took a vacation on the east coast in October of 2018. We left our cats at home and arranged to have a pet sitter tend to them. Mom loved cats. We used her nurturing ways to care for rescued kittens in the past. She was so gentle and caring with them. Naturally, I told Mom and Dad they were free to check on my cats while we were gone anytime they liked. Mom became obsessed with caring for them. Dad ended up calling me several times and ultimately asked me to tell Mom to stop going over to my house. It doesn't work that way. Mom was stuck in a loop, and nothing we could say or do would change that. It was also so sad to hear the desperation in my dad's voice. He wanted so badly for Mom to understand, but that would never be possible again.

Disorganized thinking

Alzheimer's causes one to experience difficulty with concentration, so it is natural to assume thoughts will become disorganized since they cannot concentrate on the present. We have so many experiences stored in our brain, and a healthy brain makes sense of it all and automatically produces appropriate responses. The plaques that form with Alzheimer's essentially clog up the pathways in the brain, making it difficult to connect thoughts, questions, memories and responses in a logical way. In fall of 2018, Mom stopped by after dinner, much different from her normal routine. She seemed a bit off and this was confirmed when Samantha asked which parent I got a certain trait from. I replied, "From nonno," meaning Aldo. Mom replied, "That's not true." When I asked her to explain, she said, "Because you're not his blood." Don't know who she thought I was in that moment.

Showing Mom old pictures had become very interesting by this time. She was having trouble recognizing me as a young child. She no longer understood the timing of the past. For instance, she didn't realize that I was able to know my grandfather who died when I was 18. She saw me in a picture when I was about the age of four or five, and my grandfather was in that picture. She stated, "Oh, you did get to meet your grandfather."

Here is another example of how her brain was malfunctioning. She noted a picture with me as a young adult, herself, and other relatives from Italy. My father was not in the picture. Meanwhile, Dad was explaining who the other people were when she commented that he couldn't know them because he wasn't around at that time. In her mind, because he wasn't in the picture, he didn't know them. She couldn't reconcile that I was in the picture, meaning they would've had to have been married and had a life together in order for me to be in the picture. Way too many clogged pathways preventing her from reaching that conclusion. It was truly bizarre to see her brain malfunction like this.

Simple things like processing weather became impossible. Forget showing Mom a thermostat. First, she would not remember where it was. Second, she would not remember to look at it. Third, the numbers became meaningless. One day, she asked while there was snow on the ground, "Is it hot or cold outside?"

Below is a brief conversation between mom and me.

Mom: Who are you?
Me: I'm Patty.
Mom: Where do you live?
Me: Down the block. I'm your daughter, Mom.
Mom: I know, I just haven't seen you since you were little.

To try and follow her thought process would make the strongest of us go mad.

The last dance

It was August 4th, 2018, Dad took mom to an outdoor fest at his Italian club. Festa Sotto Le Stelle translates to festival under the stars. It was a beautiful night. Jim and I stopped by later in the evening to find them dancing under the stars to some of their favorite music. They looked so happy and without a care in the world. Friends would comment on how wonderful Mom looked and that she was doing okay. Were they saying this to give us comfort, or did they feel we were exaggerating the situation? Given all the circumstances, the emotional rollercoaster, all of life's stressors, I was not in a place to appreciate what they were trying to say. All I could think of was, how dare they? How dare they presume that she is not losing her mind? My family went through a lot of terrible experiences, but to be told that she's okay was so damaging to my psyche. Sure, we did what we could to keep up appearances. To help Mom continue to experience life. Maybe help Dad feel a few precious moments of normalcy. Despite our efforts, Alzheimer's always wins. This was to be their last dance.

(Mom and dad's last dance)

Loss of place perception

In the world of healthcare, we ask orientation questions. Questions to ascertain if the patient is confused. We ask if the person knows their name, the date, where they are, and a situational question like, "Why are you in the hospital?" As a person advances through Alzheimer's and other types of dementia, they become unable to answer these questions. The person typically regresses in the opposite order I've described, meaning the first thing to go is situation. By September 2018, Mom had also lost orientation to place. She would tell Dad that she wants to visit Enzo and Laura that day. She could not understand that they lived in Italy and she was in America. From then on, Mom thought she was in Italy.

Another example to share is watching Mom trying to call her own home while using her home phone. During the next few months, it became clear that to Mom, home equated to her childhood home in Italy. However, she didn't have a phone at her childhood home, so she used the only phone number she could associate with home.

The need for 24-hour supervision

Mom was luckier than some in that she had a healthy husband who lived with her and could handle the day to day, and as mentioned earlier, Simi and I lived a short walk from one another. Had this not been the case, Mom would have had to have been institutionalized long before we did it. It was November 2018 when it became apparent that Mom could no longer be left at home even for an hour. It was a Monday, a day Simi and I covered for my dad routinely so that he could go to his Italian club. It was our way of giving him some respite. I was able to arrange to be off Mondays thanks to my co-workers who rearranged their schedules to accommodate my family's needs. Alzheimer's not only impacts the person and family but also extended family, friends, and our work lives.

On this day, our world changed again. To understand this better, let me take a step back. Mom never willingly accepted help when she perceived it to be in the form of supervision. In fact, she would rebel against it similar to how a teenager rebels. Gratefully, Alzheimer's prevented her from realizing what was happening at least for a little while. Dad would leave for the club around 1 pm and I would show up at about 1:15 and spend the day with Mom. That 15 minutes was long enough for her to dissociate Dad leaving and my arrival as two separate events. She never linked the two and was always under the impression that it was coincidence. Later on, Dad would call me to say he was on his way home. I would make sure Mom had gotten in her pajamas and cleaned up from dinner before leaving. Back when she got lost, we had installed new locks on the doors to which Mom did not have the key, so when I left, I would lock up. Dad would be expected within 30 minutes. Our plans didn't work this time; 10 minutes after I left, she was calling Dad yelling that he needed to get home and wouldn't listen. About 20 minutes after I left, she called me to say she couldn't unlock the doors because she wanted to leave to find my dad, so I went back. This was the last time Mom could be left unsupervised for even as little as 30 minutes, and the need for 24-hour supervision became a reality. It became increasingly more complicated to get Dad his respite on Mondays. I had to show up before he left and stay until after he returned home. This supervision made Mom more and more agitated, which became more and more difficult to control.

Forgetting who her family was

I took Mom on some errands to give dad a break. At the store, Mom got worried when she didn't see me and asked the greeter for help. She was never out of my sight, but she didn't see me. Her distracted brain could no longer focus. As I approached, I heard the greeter say, "Is that your sister?" and Mom acknowledging. I didn't fault Mom for those mistakes; Simi and I are similar. These statements didn't sting as much as others.

In October of 2018, my Mom asked what I do at work. Anyone who knows me for a millisecond knows I am a nurse practitioner. Being a nurse is the only thing I've ever wanted to be. It was one of the things Mom was most proud of. She would always tell the story of how I declared my future as a nurse in grammar school during an assignment that asked the students to write down "3 wishes." My first wish was to help my grandmother get better, the second was to have a pet, and the third was to become a nurse. I think the realization that Mom no longer knew what I did hit me as hard as the day she forgot who I was.

(My three wishes as written in 1977 or thereabouts)

In January of 2019, Mom said to me, "I wish I had grandchildren." Wham! Talk about being hit with a line drive right through the heart. I explained that she had 6 grandchildren, two from me and four from Rich. At that point, she chose to argue with me that Rich only had one son. In the movie *Back to the Future*, there is a scene when Michael J. Fox is holding a family photo and one by one, the members start to disappear. Now, he was able to fix the past in order to prevent that loss. Unfortunately, that's not possible with Alzheimer's. There is no going back.

On January 28th, 2019, Mom forgot who I was. It was my day to be with mom, and she was showing signs of sundowning. In patients with Alzheimer's and dementia, confusion tends to escalate when the sun goes down. This phenomenon had been creeping into our lives with more regularity every passing week, and it was becoming more pronounced and dangerous. Dangerous because the agitation can quickly escalate to violence. It was now evening, and Mom looked right at me to ask who I was. I tried reorienting her by showing her pictures of me on the wall and my driver's license, but she wouldn't believe me. She quizzed me with irrational and illogical questions. Then, she called my home and Jim answered the phone. She asked him who I was. Jim provided confirmation it was me standing there with her, and she hung up only to ask me, "What did Jim want?" She then called Jim a second time so that he could ask me to come over even though I was standing right next to Mom. Seeing my mother look at me but not see me was quite overwhelming. Not going to lie, it freaked the shit out of me. Not sure if caregivers discuss the fear they can experience as their family progresses further into the darkness. I did. I feared Mom would become physical while delusional. I feared she might attack my father unexpectedly. Nothing I read to that point had prepared me for that experience, but it was real. Hindsight clearly suggests we should have institutionalized Mom at that time.

Chapter Four: The Beginning of the End

As 2019 rolled on, Mom continued to decline. On March 1st, we had to start Mom on quetiapine, an antipsychotic used to help calm patients and get them to sleep. As far as other medications, we had decided to take Mom off the standard donepezil and memantine in 2018 with the understanding that her progression may accelerate. It was a decision we made as a family weighing the risks against the benefits. Mom had a lot of GI complaints, and we thought the medications might be contributory. It was also a fight for Dad to get her to take her meds, so under her physician's supervision, we stopped those two medications. At this point in her life, we had also taken her off of all other unnecessary medications as well and just kept her diuretic, which controlled her blood pressure very nicely. Mom was physically a healthy person. No cancer, no heart, lung, or renal disease. She did have gastric reflux, controlled hypertension, anxiety and depression. She had broken a few bones in her life and required both knee replacements, but that's it. Having to start quetiapine was a big deal and marked a decline in her status. Mom was now at stage 6. We had witnessed significant changes in her personality, which included paranoia and hallucinations. She became highly suspicious of our interactions. Without supervision, Mom would wear multiple layers of clothing, and she would forget who my father was. We had the medication on hand in anticipation for this day. When I went to their house, I found Mom agitated, yelling that this man was not her husband. She was visibly upset, exhausted and confused. Horrible and heart-crushing to watch.

One of the harder lessons to learn is that whatever you plan, it isn't going to work. Dad and I would come up with an updated plan weekly, but Mom had other plans for us. She kept throwing us curve balls. Dad would call while he was at his club to ask me how things were going. Mom picked up on the fact that this was not normal behavior for us and correctly accused me of "babysitting" her. It became more and more difficult to help Mom calm down once agitated. On this particular Monday, Mom became upset and told me to leave, yet I stayed. She would walk up and down the hallway and repeatedly ask me to leave, but I would not / could not do so for her safety. Sensing her agitation, I locked the door. She then called Dad to yell at him, stating that I was being mean and that he should come home. After the phone call to Dad, she called Jim. Suddenly, she flipped a switch and she now believed I was my own daughter. She demanded that Jim pick her (me) up. Once off the phone with Jim and without satisfactory resolution, she decided to call my cell phone while I was in the kitchen standing next to her. It was then she regained her senses about who I was and completely forgot she had originally been upset about "babysitting." The events did create more confusion for her, and by the end of the night, she was mad at my father. What a rollercoaster. It wasn't long after we started quetiapine that Mom could no longer make phone calls because she couldn't seem to dial correctly anymore. She had made her last phone call.

It Is Not a Urinary Tract Infection

We would discuss these events with our physician. Oftentimes, we were given generic answers like, "Maybe she has a UTI". Older adults are tested frequently for urinary tract infections (UTIs). Whether or not Alzheimer's patients have UTIs was very much a question in my mind. Is hygiene problematic at this stage? Yes. Can the patient be expected to collect a clean sample? No. People with normal immune systems are able to fend off common bacterial colonizations without suffering infection. Yet, with every dirty sample, Mom would be put on another course of antibiotics. Not saying there aren't people who suffer recurrent UTIs, but these begin much earlier in life and are confirmed by cultures. This was not the case with my mom. Regardless, blaming a UTI became modus operandi when describing increased confusion to healthcare providers and friends. Can increased confusion be a sign of a UTI? Yes, but confusion is only one symptom of many associated with UTIs as well as a symptom associated with many other diagnoses. Ultimately, I refused to have Mom's urine tested anymore. Was I right or wrong? All I can say is that Mom never suffered so much as a fever.

Delusional thinking

If you look up delusion, the definition is a false belief regarding an external reality held despite irrefutable evidence to the contrary. By April of 2019, Mom's delusions were a daily occurrence. She would call my dad's cell phone while he stood right in front of her yet she still did not believe he was Aldo. On April 13th, 2019, Dad called me for help stating Mom was out of control yet again. Jim and I walked over to find Mom yelling and stomping about the house and crying inconsolably. This time, she was demanding that this man (my father) leave immediately. Dad and Jim went down to the basement to give me time to work with Mom. After a while, Mom seemed to calm down so I went to check on Dad. He was obviously disturbed by this behavior but it was now to the point where he was more aggravated than upset. He and Jim were watching television, so I went back upstairs and discovered that Mom had climbed out the living room window and was walking down the street. I quickly caught up to her and re-directed her towards my house. Mom was still very upset from the delusion that there was a stranger in her home stating, "I can't go back to that house where that stranger is!" She and I hadn't been at my home for more than 5 minutes when she said she wanted to return home. We walked back and as soon as she saw my dad, she had a smile on and told him she was happy he was back.

First Hospital Admission

Mom had continued to decline. We continued tweaking medications, but none of them made a difference. It got to the point where Mom was crying all the time. We reached our first breaking point on May 15th, 2019. For the past month, Mom had complained of abdominal pain and being cold and tired. Just when we start to worry, she would literally jump up, eat like a horse, and become agitated. The distressed calls from Dad were now occurring multiple times per day. On this particular day, Mom awoke with her now typical "attack" of belly pain. Once it subsided, Dad thought he could get away with a trip to the nursery. He and Mom took the drive together. Dad, still not understanding the way her disease works, left her in the car. After returning from buying his plants, he found Mom confused, crying and throwing things around in the car. I decided it was time for another doctor visit, who decided it was time for an admission. Mom was admitted to rule out any acute abdominal processes, of which there were none, but also for a psychiatric evaluation. I remember getting up to the room. Staff were so nice to us. They gave us a very nice room at the end of the hall. Unfortunately, it was at the end of the hall. I did explain to the staff that Mom would need some closer observation. That first night was traumatic for everyone. Dad was afraid to leave. Mom went nuts. I had to talk Dad off the ledge. Mom called me, asking me to bring her home. Security had to restrain her. This scene would repeat itself the following night. Mom had been moved to a room across from the nurse's station within a few hours of admission. It was so sad to watch. Mom did not understand what was happening to her and why we couldn't take her home. She kept telling me I would be punished. At this point, there was no good option. It was only torture for everyone, but worst of all, Mom. I am so sorry, Mom; I wished it wasn't like this. I wished I knew how to help you.

(Mom would cry often at this stage and was inconsolable at times. She was
not able to express why she would cry either. We felt helpless.)

On May 16th, a psychiatrist met with Mom. His questions upset her to the point that she told him to go away. She even hit his hand away after he extended it for a handshake. I followed him and asked if a geriatric psychiatry (gero-psych) admission would be appropriate. He said no. When he said Mom did not meet criteria, I felt lost and at the end of my rope. How were we going to take her home? We had fixed nothing! Gero-psych admissions are intended for people with disturbed thinking and dementia who need behavior modification medications and stabilization. These medications are potent and, therefore, require close supervision and frequent adjustments. The patients are observed to ensure the desired effect is achieved. It is not a good place to be, but it often becomes necessary in this population.

On May 17th, we met with a psychiatric nurse practitioner whom I've known for several years. I have always valued her service to our hospital. The nurse practitioner called me to discuss Mom's behavior. She concluded that Mom's condition was swinging between two states, two polars if you will. When she was in her low state, she would cry, complain of abdominal pains, and feel tired and cold. She would then flip into her "manic" phase, which would manifest as agitation, hallucinations, and confusion. It was then we realized her abdominal pain was psychosomatic. Contrary to the evaluation from the previous day, the NP thought Mom would benefit from a gero-psych admission. I immediately felt overwhelming relief. A huge weight had been lifted. Later that evening, Mom became increasingly restless. She didn't understand why she couldn't go home. Dad stayed with her until 8 pm when visiting hours were over. At 9:30 pm, the nurse called me to report Mom's level of agitation and asked that I return to the hospital. Not even the 1:1 sitter could keep her in her room. I did return to the hospital, and Mom was indeed quite upset. There was not much for me to do except try to redirect. A bed on the psychiatric ward became available at 11 pm.

Admission to the psychiatric ward proved extremely difficult for both Mom and me. It was the best of bad choices, but that didn't make it hurt less. I could tell Mom was exhausted from the last few days and was now somewhat subdued. She readily followed staff to her new room. My attention turned to the patients in the hallway. One man was in a wheelchair bent over and picking things off the ground that didn't exist. A woman was wandering aimlessly around the hallway. Another more fragile-appearing woman was secured in what would equate to an adult highchair, sitting quietly staring at nothing. That's when it all hit me. My mom, the psychiatric ward, the realization that her disease had progressed to the point of needing institutionalization. Once Mom was escorted to her room, and a nurse began asking me intake questions, I felt my eyes fill with tears and a lump form in my throat. I couldn't muster any words, instead just nodded yes and no. The nurse offered me a place to stay while Mom was being checked in, but I couldn't. I was too upset. I wasn't strong enough to put my feelings aside and be there for Mom. I left the ward and found myself walking towards where I work in the ICU. It had been my workplace for almost 28 years. Maybe my feet took me there because it was so familiar, maybe because it was routine, maybe because I wanted to forget why I was at the hospital. Once at the nurse's station, I saw some familiar faces and collapsed into tears. I literally dropped to my knees and wept openly. The staff in the office were kind enough to let me grieve. Retrospectively, I think this is when I grieved the loss of my mother.

A few weeks passed while providers attempted to find a medication regimen that would keep Mom calm, yet awake. On this particular day, Mom was very calm but very altered. She was not making sense. It was like twisted dreams became a reality. For instance, she thought she was baking bread and one loaf was bigger than the others and then a dog jumped out of it. She used to make bread weekly back in the day, and we had a dog named Dino. Her mind must have combined the memories into what her mind saw now. Her stream of consciousness was so perverse that it was difficult to follow. Every now and again, a true memory would surface, and I could join the conversation once again.

Another behavior that fascinated me was when she would write notes to her mother and father both who had passed away decades before. The notes were written as if she were in her teen years. One said something to the effect that she and Simi were together and her mother didn't need to pick them up. As if she left a note on the kitchen table for her mother to find.

The psychiatrist would check in with me regularly. The process to stabilize Mom was arduous. The physician would make a change to her medications and observe her behavior. Every change required 24 to 48 hours of observation. The agitation was easier to control, but her deep-seated depression was a bit more complicated. Mom would not eat and repeatedly told the psychiatrist she wanted to die. Enter more guilt. You see, a few months ago, when Mom's agitation was getting worse, her medical doctor suggested an anit-psychotic med, one that may have adverse consequences if used in combination with her antidepressant. Together, we agreed it would be best to stop the anti-depressant. Fast forward to now, and my retrospective glasses were showing me this was not a good plan. What I should have done was take Mom to a psychiatrist instead. I was angry with myself that I hadn't thought of that on my own. While I could rationalize with myself that Mom's behavior was worsening and it would reach this point regardless of more specialists, the guilt was heavy. To make up for the guilt, I hoped that we could bring Mom home again before she needed admission to memory care.

Bringing Mom Home

As it was getting closer to Mom's discharge, we needed to make some more changes to the house. Jim put stops on the windows so she couldn't crawl out anymore. He installed a lock on the basement door so Mom would have to stay on the main floor. We did this for her safety as well as for my Dad's sanity. You see, she was moving everything, and it was a huge source of frustration for Dad. He would buy things, and then she would lose them. Nothing was safe. She would even hide or destroy the bills. With the door locked, Dad could keep all of his items safe. I enlisted the help of my daughters to help declutter the house. My mom's house, once meticulously clean and kept, was now a victim of obsessive behavior. Mom had stored multiple plastic containers in every closet. Unused wrapping paper was in every corner. She had multiple soaps on the bathroom counter. We minimized everything. Mom had taken to applying different perfumes multiple times daily. It got to the point that it was difficult to be in the same room with her because the cologne was so strong. Most of her colognes were put away, and we only left one out. Another item was razors. I believed my mom stopped using a razor many years ago, yet I found over 50 in her bathroom. We also collected all loose photographs to store safely in the basement and got rid of all the Scotch tape. I found myself wondering if Mom had underlying psychiatric disorders all along. With her brain no longer providing cover, we could see the obsessions, the anxiety, and depression so clearly. It made other things clear, like how my brother and I were never able to touch anything and our rooms always had to be in perfect order. I thought it was an Italian thing, but it may have been much more than culture. The last item to prepare was obtaining a caregiver. Dad and I decided to start with twice weekly coverage.

On June 6th, Mom was discharged home. Dad was on the phone with me within 90 minutes of arrival, and he was already struggling. He was openly frustrated and crying. He kept repeating, "I don't know what to do." Thank God Simi was home and able to help him get organized. Where was I? At work, insert more guilt. The thought of taking a leave of absence was a daily thought in my head. But this would not be like a maternity leave or surgical leave with a defined endpoint. There was no endpoint in sight. Not to mention, I know myself and know that I would not be able to care for Mom as she needed. I wasn't strong enough. Rich was scheduled to come for a visit in a few weeks. For this I was grateful and used the time to make plans for Mom.

My cousin Andy called me on June 10th. His mom, my aunt Franca, had been admitted to memory care a few years before. Andy shared stories about his mom's behavior before she was admitted. While I thought Mom was unique, he told me stories that showed the exact same behavior that Franca exhibited. It was mind-blowing to know that both sisters were tortured by the same demons. Andy did acknowledge that Nara was progressing very quickly through her later stages compared to Franca. After the call, I remember feeling good about taking Mom home and that we could forge ahead, a short-lived euphoric moment.

The week that followed solidified the reality that we needed to admit Mom to memory care. I can't describe the amount of inner conflict I felt during this time. Just imagine your father calling you and saying, "You have to put her away." Bringing Mom home from the hospital wasn't a good plan. Simi and I had to go rescue the situation daily. Our first caregiver day went horribly wrong and ended up with the caregiver quitting. Mom continued to demand to return to Tiglio (her childhood home). Never mind that Tiglio had not been her home since 1957. When I asked how old she was, mom said she was 21. This marked the end of time perception. Mom was only oriented to herself at this point, meaning she was entering the final stages of Alzheimer's. It is indescribable to watch how contorted her thought process had become. The awkward smile, the nervous picking, the attempt to keep up social cues. About 80% of the time, Mom only recognized me as someone she knew but no longer equated me as her daughter. Cherished was that remaining 20%.

(Wrapping a framed picture with a blanket and attempting to secure it with a metal tape measure.)

The next Monday, I found myself at the Walmart pharmacy at 8:30 pm because my dad neglected to tell me we were out of lorazepam. Lorazepam is a sedative. Mom would become more agitated when the sun went down as is a phenomenon that happens to most in her condition. We had a supply of Ativan to help my dad get her to relax, but not this night. Of course, nothing was easy. There were no refills, the physician's office was closed, and I had to wait for the answering service to reach the doctor and then for the doctor to speak to the pharmacist.

Right about now was when I put down the deposit to hold Mom's memory care reservation. Later, we sent notification that we were anticipating admission within 2 weeks. Next, I ran around to pick up essentials for mom's new apartment, being mindful of what she would consider normal albeit her normal was based on where she thought she was in any given moment.

Strange behavior continued. Mom has taken to "packing" all of her remaining clothing in tall white kitchen garbage bags because she was convinced she was going home.

I watched as Mom wrapped a picture frame in a baby blanket and secured it with a safety pin then tried to tie it with a tape measure. She obsessed about death and believed her parents were missing. It was like she couldn't wake up from a bad dream. Dad continued to argue with her, even now. Want to know something else that's crazy? I continued to tell Dad to stop.

We had a good idea on where we would place Mom. Dad and I were getting all the required documents together. Next, Mom would need to be evaluated and wait for the admission to be approved. We were thinking it might have been within the next week. No one could believe how fast the cognitive decline had been for Mom. One year ago, we celebrated their 60th anniversary with friends and family. This year, Mom will be admitted to memory care where she will spend the rest of her life. She will no longer be able to live at home, sleep in her bed, watch television in her favorite chair. I looked at Mom and saw a shell of who she once was. While she was still physically strong, she was also scared and tortured and sad. I saw a person who had no capacity to understand what was happening, nor could she see what was to come. We were about to uproot her from what little remained familiar and traumatize her with a strange environment surrounded by strange people. I kept trying to reassure myself that Alzheimer's patients live in the moment, and while that did bring me some peace, it did not prevent me from waking at 4 am to journal these feelings at the time.

Back to the caregiver notion we had. Mom would not accept the second person who was sent from the agency. She yelled at her to go away. She told Dad that she would strangle her if she didn't leave. Simi and I tried to take her on a walk, but we didn't get more than 2 houses away before she wanted to turn back. She kept insisting that my dad would leave her behind. No amount of reasoning mattered; we were just risking our own sanity by trying to redirect her. I opened the door to the home and let Mom in. As soon as I locked and closed the door, Mom reopened it. I found myself fighting with her, pulling the door shut because I didn't want to deal with it (her) anymore. How messed up is that? I caved and let her reopen the door, at which point she reached over to give me a kiss goodbye. More guilt. Simi and I went back to her place to chat a while. She was so supportive during these God-awful times despite the fact she needed support herself. This was her sister. I was only thinking of myself. More guilt. Simi and I hadn't been alone for too long before Dad called with his predictable, "I don't know what to do!" So I walked back to their home and found Mom outside. I watched as Mom was grieving someone's death yet again. At first it was her mother, then some man that knew her grandmother. Then she became angry because we wouldn't take her home. Then she started screaming. Ultimately, she succumbed to the sedative. This day was over, only to be repeated tomorrow.

Another reality I learned about Alzheimer's along the way is that it changes your senses. You might think you see with your eyes and hear with your ears, but Alzheimer's is strong enough to overpower even your senses. To Mom, I could be her daughter, mother, sister, granddaughter, or sometimes a childhood friend. It all would depend on what her mind saw in that moment. Recently, she called me thinking I was her mother. I played along but had to break "character" to fill in the Italian dialogue with an English word or phrase. Didn't matter. She heard her mother's voice. Alzheimer's will also twist feelings of hunger. Mom would skip entire meals and state she was full with all she ate.

(June 22nd, Simi hosted a dinner for us. It would be Mom's last family dinner outside of memory care. Even though Mom was especially out of sorts that day, I will forever be grateful for the memory. Left to right: Garry (Simi's son), Rich, Andy (Franca's son), Dad, Mom, Simi and I'm in the back.)

It was now June 23rd, 2019, and I still found myself struggling with the decision to admit mom to memory care. I was tortured by guilt every day and every night. Rich traveled in yesterday. His presence was enough to keep Mom on the good end of the bad spectrum. Without saying so much, I felt Rich believed we could still manage Mom at home. Especially if Dad could learn to work with her.

I tried to look at the big picture. On the pro side of admitting Mom to memory care, she would live in a more suitable and safer environment. She would be supervised by specially trained staff who get to go home after their shift to recharge, unlike my family. She would be more closely observed by a psychiatrist. A nurse would manage her medications. There were more people available to intervene when she became agitated. My father, Simi, Jim, Rich, and I could go back to living our lives and process this trauma to move on. Finally, the reality that this was a progressive and relentless disease that will not stop. Mom would require more and more assistance as time went by. On the con side is my brain. I felt like I was giving up a child for adoption. A child too young to understand why but old enough to feel abandoned. My guilt in this situation came from a place that told me it was my responsibility to care for my mother. Caring for your parent should come above all else, even work and my family. While this was my culture, I knew myself and believed I would quickly resent this role nor would I be able to fulfill it in a way that would keep my mother stable. Mom and her sisters took care of my grandmother when she became wheelchair-bound and demented. The three of them would split the day into 3 shifts so my grandfather could still do what he needed to do. This was what my mother and father would say was my job. Not directly, but again, based on our culture. Jim tried to make me feel better by explaining that Mom was never "home" anymore. That place in her mind no longer existed.

Admission day was approaching. Rich had traveled back home but sent me this note.

I don't think I have said it enough to you how grateful I am that you were here as strong as you have been weathering this storm. But let me say it again "Thank you." Regarding the decision I am 100% on board with it. Let there be no doubt in your mind. She is too much to handle. I took her out this afternoon for a drive. We went down the alley at 6718. MISTAKE. That was home! She unbuckled her seat belt and was ready to get out. I told her I forgot the keys and had to go back to get them. I wish I could be here for you next Monday. It won't be easy. I also believe you will sense a feeling of relief however small over this situation. She will be cared for in a way that we could not provide at home. That is not an admission of failure or lack of trying. We all knew this day was coming. BTW I'm Gabriele right now. I love you Patty. Thanks to Jim also. He has put up with a lot.

Rich would have no idea how much Jim would actually have to put up with just two days later.

June 25th, Dad continued to call incessantly. I knew this was hard on him, but we were less than a week away from admission. I could not concentrate on any work that I had to do. Mom became extremely agitated when the new caregiver arrived. This day would deteriorate to a new low. Mom made a run for it and came to my house with the caregiver chasing after her. Jim was home and found Mom sitting on our couch upset, hyperventilating, telling him some story in Italian. He gathered that she thought the caregiver was trying to hurt her. Jim tried talking to the caregiver at our back door, who was also extremely upset. Meanwhile, Mom escaped out the front door and ran across the street to the neighbor's home. She rang their bell and then forced her way into their home as soon as they opened it. She literally pushed her way past the homeowner to gain entry to the home. She then accused the homeowner of knowing the caregiver. By this time, Jim had run over and convinced Mom to go home with him. How do I know all this happened? The neighbor had a front door camera that recorded the entire event. This generated about fifteen more calls and texts while I was at work, and so I left early to go assess the situation. Things calmed down, and Simi had come over to help again. It was at this point Simi reported that Dad had forgotten to give mom her scheduled sedative. Knowing I had three clinical shifts in a row, I begged my dad to call Simi for help instead of me so I could concentrate on my patients.

June 26th, the day the bomb went off. Radio silence for the morning. Regardless, this whole situation was heavy on my mind. Around 1 pm, I got a text from Simi, "We are in the Emergency Department." What the fuck! Mom started the day with her new normal demands, "I want to go home," first thing in the morning. At some point, Dad took her for a ride in the car to distract her, something he had found useful over the past few weeks. Mom kept insisting he take her home. Dad wanted her to tell him where to go, and the two of them kept going back and forth. Mom's agitation escalated, and Dad's patience ran out. Disastrous combination. Mom attempted to exit the moving car. Dad struggled to keep her from jumping out and decided to pull her hair in an attempt to restrain her. Mom now felt assaulted and fought more. Dad continued to drive. He headed over to Simi's house where he finally parked the car to call for help. Simi was out running errands and headed back immediately to find Dad physically restraining Mom while she was screaming and hitting my father. Simi called 911.

Mom was calm and cheerful when I saw her in the emergency room. Dad saw me and stated, "Did Simi call you? I didn't call you." More guilt. Regardless, I unleashed some anger on my father and scolded him for not pulling over to call the police himself. He made excuses, but I did not let him win. He could have gotten them both killed or taken out innocent bystanders. Needless to say, Mom was readmitted to gero-psych and would discharge directly to memory care. That was the last morning she woke up at home.

Second Hospital Admission

This admission was less traumatic for all of us. We were used to the routine. It was a few days into the admission when I got a call from Mom. It went something like this:

Aldo left, but is coming back.
Nonno is fine.
Lawnmower doesn't work.
Others are hitting me with a ball.
I'm still at Gloria's, will probably stay here for dinner.

Simi came back with the little one.
I told Gloria I can't watch the kids anymore.
If I didn't have my mom, I would be in bed all day.
Something happened to the priest.
Patty, go to bed and stay warm.
Eva is helping with the kids.
Patty let the dog out and put him in a tube, but he's okay.

While it was sad to listen to her flight of ideas, in her mind, she was with all of us. Meanwhile, the psychiatrist wanted to add yet another medication because she was still too restless. Mom looked tired and defeated. She now assumed the posture of the other more advanced patients. Her head leaned forward, back slightly bent, mask-like face at times. All effects of medications required to quiet her mind. On this day, Mom let Dad and me go home without a fight. It was so hard watching her slip away into oblivion.

On July 1st, Dad and I went to memory care to sign the contract for Mom's admission. I was asking the director questions about doctor visits when my dad asked if Mom would still be seeing our family doctor. I said no because she would not be able to leave memory care to see him. Mom would be followed by the resident physician. To lighten things up, I made a joke about driving Mom anywhere after their last car ride. I believed this was the moment the finality set in with Dad. He broke down into tears, and a second time after he saw the apartment. After 61 years together, they would no longer live in the same home, and it was not because of death or divorce. It is a dreadful disease that steals your everything. Mom would never feed my rabbit again, or walk down my street. Mom would never sleep in the same room with my father again. Holidays would have an empty seat. Our lives were forever changed.

For those of you unfamiliar with the cost of memory care, let me enlighten you. It is not enough to worry about how or who will care for Mom when you can no longer do it. If the burden of the disease alone isn't enough to break you, the cost of memory care certainly will. When we were researching choices, the average monthly cost was $6,000 to $8,000 per month. Some facilities wanted to nickel and dime us with essentials like diapers and the luxury of having Mom bathed by a patient care tech once per week. All your assets would be used to pay for room and board. My father, like many in his generation, was the sole provider living on a modest income. Mom and Dad did not have big investments or retirement plans. Also like most people his age, Dad was on a fixed income. Andy was in a similar situation and found a good option for my aunt Franca but had to take her out of the state. So again, was it not enough to concentrate on the disease and provide safe and effective care to our loved ones? No, it was not. My advice is to seek an elder attorney if your loved one is advancing through Alzheimer's.

We did what we could with the money we had and knew some day, when the money ran out, Mom would have to be transferred to a Medicaid facility. The thought of that was always on my mind. The facility we chose had a Medicaid building, but there was a waiting list. When we first signed the admission papers, we were told the average wait time was 6 to 12 months. We thought we would have enough funds to get us through. From time to time, I would ask the administrator where Mom was on the waiting list, only to be ignored or provided a vague answer. The question I always got in return was, "Approximately where is the family with funds?" What options would we have as the money ran out? Well, I put some thoughts down on paper for my dad and brother to consider. One, look for a Medicaid facility immediately so Dad could stay in his home longer. Two, find a facility that could provide senior living for my dad in one section, and memory care in another for Mom. You would be surprised that this is a valid option. Three, sell the family home and move Dad into a condo to have more money for Mom in her current location. We decided we would ultimately sell the family home and move Dad to a condo. This real-estate project was put on hold until we knew we would only have 4 to 6 months of payments left.

During my visit with Mom on July 7th, she complained that her neck was stiff. I asked staff for a hot pack, which helped, and I went on my way. I was called as soon as I left by the staff who reported that Mom bit open the pack and they presumed she ate some of the pellets because they were on her face. Poison control was called, and staff asked our rapid response team to look at her. It was always something.

It was now July 8th, Mom's 82nd birthday, celebrated on the gero-psych ward. The psychiatrist informed me that Mom would need to stay a few more days. It was good news to hear that he was not making any further medication adjustments for now. I probed for information regarding Mom's rapid decline. He explained that Mom had both Alzheimer's and vascular dementia. Vascular dementia is responsible for the rapid decline, but typically the patient will plateau prior to another step down. Mom beat the odds; we did not enjoy any plateaus her last 2 years of life. Her sister Franca had Alzheimer's exclusively, which explained why she was progressing more steadily through the stages. To complicate Mom, she suffered from severe anxiety and depression most of her life. Not helpful. I made an appointment with Palliative care services to talk about her future so I could be more prepared for what was to come.

Chapter Five: Admission to Memory care

What an exhausting ride the last 2 years had been. Move-in day finally arrived. On July 11th, Mom was admitted to memory care where she would spend her remaining time on earth. She was now on five different medications, and they seem to multiply. She had started to retain water because her diuretic had been held due to low blood pressure. She was not sleeping. She looked miserable. I prayed for the end of her life. Is that wrong?

Dad and I decided to give Mom a few days to acclimate to her new environment. This was suggested to us by the director of the facility. It made sense at the time. When Dad, Simi and I visited for the first time on July 14th, we found Mom in a wheelchair wearing an adult diaper. The medications had pummeled her into submission. Her legs were full of edema, so much so that she required bigger shoes. Her bathroom was smeared with feces. Staff told us she refused to accept help. Simi and I showered my mother and cleaned the bathroom. My heart was broken. What had I done?

A few weeks passed, and we found a routine. We no longer got phone calls from Mom. We didn't have to keep her busy. We didn't have to worry about what she was going to break or if she would fall down the stairs any longer. On our next visit, Dad and I sat with Mom in the common room where she decided to take off her top. It was so weird seeing my mom's bare chest in a public setting. She undressed without inhibitions. Who was this person who looked like my mom? Dad still didn't understand how to interact with Mom. He wanted to direct her like he had done their entire marriage instead of working with her thoughts and needs in the moment.

A week later, I received a call from the nurse who asked if it was ok to add a 6th and 7th medication for stabilization. When I asked why, I was told she could be aggressive at times. This was the first time I was hearing this and instinctively said no. But I did instruct the nurse to get the opinion of the psychiatrist. That backfired. That night, a different nurse called and told me the psychiatrist might be recommending another gero-psych admission. The thought of going back to gero-psych hit me like a brick. My head started spinning with what this would do to Mom. I waited for word from the psychiatrist the next day. The nurse practitioner called me and reported that

Mom was not aggressive in the least bit. In fact, Mom gave her a hug. She and I reviewed her medications, and we settled on increasing one in lieu of starting another. No gero-psych.

Another sign of Decline in Alzheimer's, as discussed previously, is incontinence. However, the problem at earlier stages was that patients did not recognize the urge to have a bowel movement. Currently, Mom was forgetting where it was appropriate to have that bowel movement. Given their developmental age regressed as they progressed through the stages, I assimilated this behavior to when my kids were potty training and they would hide when it was time to poop. Soon, she would no longer know when it was happening at all.

Mom started falling. Eventually, Alzheimer's patients become bedbound. Mom was fighting her weakness with everything she had. Couple this with a boatload of psychiatric medications and voila, recurrent falls. The facility was required to send Mom to the local emergency department after every unwitnessed fall if they suspected injury. Basically, every time. In fact, she fell 3 times within the first month, and by August, she fell 3 times in 3 days. At this point, I felt we should talk about hospice. Mom didn't want to live like this, but I also didn't know if she would meet criteria.

Goals of care

The phrase "goals of care" is what we use to label discussions that are to define what a person would accept as their death nears. Some people want everything done to prolong their life. Others will accept the natural disease process without allowing medicine to interfere. Most of us fall somewhere in the middle. Mom, for instance, took good care of her physical self. She was an avid walker. Her diet was pretty healthy, never smoked, and alcohol was minimal. She followed doctor's orders and completed all recommended screening. When she had to have her knees replaced, she did her rehab without a fight. However, Mom was clear that she never wanted machines to keep her alive, nor did she want to live with Alzheimer's. Not everyone gets enough warning to invoke hospice. What I often see is hospice being chosen when the patient has only a few hours or days to live. As someone nears the end of life, hospice can help both the patient and family achieve peace.

Before discussing hospice, I think it is important to discuss resuscitation. I work in an intensive care unit. Death surrounds me, so I can speak about it more frankly. I can also speak to the futility of providing CPR when it is not indicated. Cardiopulmonary resuscitation was invented to pump the heart in patients who have suffered a heart attack in an effort to give time for revascularization of clogged arteries. You have a 20% chance of surviving a cardiac arrest within a hospital setting, even in critical care. Your odds are worse if your heart stops at home or anywhere else. Over the years, patients and families have been given the option to choose CPR in the event the heart stops regardless of the cause. What I think the general public doesn't understand is that CPR is not a cure. It may restart the heart, but it does not reverse the reason it stopped in the first place. When you have a patient in the final stages of Alzheimer's, when you know there is no cure, when all of their dignity has been taken from them, why would you want to restart their heart? Why would you selfishly want to keep them alive only to live in their nightmare longer? Mom was made a do-not-resuscitate when she was first admitted to gero-pysch, and I never once regretted it. Let me take one step back. Mom and Dad had a living will long before she was diagnosed with Alzheimer's. Oftentimes, families confuse this with a do not resuscitate order. Living wills are to tell the healthcare team who the surrogate decision maker is and what the person is willing to accept in the way of healthcare. The decision to make a person a do-not-resuscitate is distinct from a living will, but the living will provides direction. The do-not-resuscitate is a portable physician order that tells healthcare providers it is the patient's and/or surrogates' decision to allow natural death. Families I talk to at work often think these are one and the same.

Enter hospice as a concept. Hospice can be considered when the focus of care for someone with an incurable or irreversible condition would shift from treatment to comfort. We would simply allow nature to take its course. If Mom fell, she would not require the obligatory trip to the emergency department. If Mom fell and had a traumatic injury, we could seek medical attention if that would make her more comfortable. It just depends. One of the criteria for hospice in patients is weight loss. Mom began a slow but noticeable drop in weight after admission to memory care. Her edema resolved, and weight started coming off. Dad would visit every day and feed her lunch. Staff would offer snacks every two hours, but none of that mattered. The weight was coming off. Not to mention the frequent falls. On August 28th, 2019, Mom took another tumble that left her with a black eye. On August 29th, 2019, we enrolled Mom in hospice, and I mourned another step.

(Mom with a black eye)

A few months went by with signs of deterioration appearing unapologetically. As the holidays approached, we attempted to stave off the grief by planning to dine with Mom at her facility. I remember our Thanksgiving meal but not Christmas. I think that is because I really didn't want this to be reality. Meanwhile, Sonia was expecting her first child. A baby girl who was due on my birthday in February. Over New Year's, Sonia was starting to have contractions. In fact, she spent New Year's Eve in the hospital for observation. On January 3rd, 2020, my first granddaughter was born. Caroline made her entry prematurely but was strong nonetheless. People talk about the love you feel as a grandparent, and I finally felt what all the hoopla was about. There are no words to describe the pure joy you feel.

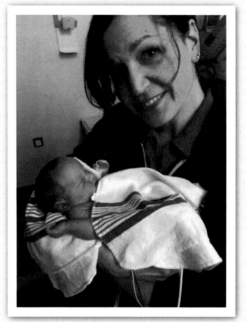

(Holding my first grandchild for the first time. It was love at first sight and a welcome distraction.)

During my visit on January 25th, I had Mom sit at the piano in one of the common areas. Let me back up a bit. My parents' neighbors make a living by teaching music lessons and tuning pianos. They visited Mom early in her stay. Mr. Chung assessed the piano and realized it was significantly out of tune. He was so very gracious and tuned the piano at the facility free of charge. He knew Nara and understood how much playing the piano meant to her. Mom had always been able to continue playing. Dad and I were often in awe of her ability to play, but Alzheimer's took that away too. As Mom sat on the piano bench, she very weakly pressed several keys. No melody, no song, just random keys. This would be the last time Mom would sit at a piano.

By February of 2020, mom had lost over 25 pounds, rarely spoke, and we would find her in the common room in the quasi-catatonic state shared by the majority of tenants. Her jaw was in constant motion, a side effect of the medications. When she was too tired, her mouth just hung open. Dad was elated that she was calm. I saw this as another loss. As March approached, it became evident that we would need to downsize Dad both to free more funds for Mom and simplify life for him as homeownership was proving problematic. In February 2020, we listed my parents' home for sale.

(January 25th, 2020: Nara's last attempt to play piano. She hit random keys and then began brushing them as if to attempt a glissando. Only a small portion of the key hits were strong enough to produce sound.)

Do you see what I see?

Some time in February I was contacted by hospice. The nurse informed me that Mom may not meet criteria be considered hospice worthy any longer. My jaw must have hit the ground with a loud thud, because the nurse then asked if I disagreed with that assessment. I replied with a resounding "YES." My mentor, colleague and dear friend has taught me many lessons throughout my career as a nurse practitioner. One of which is the understanding that perception is reality. The catch phrase "do you see what I see" was used frequently on shift. This lesson applied to both providers and families. For example, a patient would come in to my unit at the ripe old age of 98. Unable to walk or talk or eat without the assistance of a tube that passes directly through the abdominal wall to the stomach. This patient would be suffering from heart, lung, and renal disease and present with an acute infection. Sepsis is a common final pathway for many. What I can never get used to is the family's reaction to our attempts to suggest the end of their loved one's life is approaching. A common response is "I don't understand, they were fine yesterday." I don't fault families for this perception. They don't always see the forest through the trees. The decline may have been so gradual that it went unnoticed. It is my job to help them accept the concept of death. The same denial, if you will, goes for some healthcare providers. Specialty consultants will speak to the families from a narrowed perspective. Meaning, it is possible for say the kidneys to recover after the critical illness has resolved but that does not mean the patient will regain their memory and re-establish their independence. No, what we have done is prolong the dying process with treatments for acute illness in a terminal patient.

In my mom's case, the hospice nurse had not personally evaluated Nara for some time. She was reliant on nursing reports. She cited that Mom hadn't fallen in over a month, but did not understand Mom was no longer walking unassisted. Again, no one's fault. People have a tendency to report things in a positive light. It would be easy for me to imagine the conversation between the hospice nurse and memory care nurse as follows:

Hospice: Anything new to report for Nara?
Memory care: She hasn't fallen in several weeks, and has been able to sit in the day room
for longer periods
Hospice: Let me know if you notice any changes.

Without asking specific questions, ongoing weight loss, limited mobility and lack of speech would not be reported. I couldn't help but think to myself "do you see what I see?" I was able to outline these observations which meant Mom did in fact continue to meet criteria for hospice.

Quarantine

In December 2019, Wuhan, China, announced they were battling a new contagion. By March 2020, the world was facing the COVID-19 pandemic. Memory care closed its doors to visitors, as did all these types of facilities. Mom was on her own. Dad would try calling, but Mom could no longer make coherent conversation nor could she stay focused. The facility would allow visitation behind glass, but this did not work out for us. Dad was trying to smile and blow kisses to Mom when Mom started screaming for him and got agitated. It was times like that when I felt as though Mom still had periods of lucidity. I believe she did. Moments when she woke up and realized that she was not at home and was scared or sad or angry and then slipped back into the fog of her disease.

Where was I during this plague? Working as a nurse practitioner in a critical care unit barely holding on. My team worked day after day. Weeks and shifts went on forever. Some providers chose to live in a hotel so as not to infect their families. I would change into scrubs at work and dispose of them prior to leaving my shift. I slept in my guest room for months, afraid I would pass on the disease to my family.

Our approach to providing care for this population changed constantly. We had no large randomized controlled studies to guide our decisions. We relied heavily on each other as a healthcare community. My medical director created a consortium that brought providers from our entire healthcare system together virtually via a weekly conference to discuss and share what was working and what was not. Best practice was re-defined daily. These were unprecedented times.

We resorted to basic means to communicate in the patient care areas. The healthcare team would don their isolation gear and cluster care. We utilized the glass doors and paper towels to write messages or keep notes. This level of isolation precautions would last 21 days per patient. During the first weeks, our hospital assigned nursing staff to be monitors. These nurses had the sole responsibility to monitor how we donned and doffed our gear. Obviously, we did not have the resources to keep that up very long as the number of afflicted grew. I distinctly remember chuckling about that because I felt like it was a waste of a good nurse.

(Nurses would gown up and spend 20-30 minutes in a room at a time. Staff would communicate with signs or by writing on the glass to avoid opening the doors and increase exposure. In this picture, you can see the sign "No CPR." At no other time is it ok to communicate something as intimate as your code status on a hand written piece of paper taped to the door with medical tape for the world to see. These were the worst of times during the pandemic.)

No one escaped unscathed. I watched as the strongest of nurses and doctors crumbled with exhaustion and heartbreak. Death surrounded us daily. It was hideous. Families had to say goodbye virtually. We would admit patients and do what we could to keep them off life-support because we knew about 80% of those would die, and so many patients required life support. We cried all day, every day. We watched helplessly with agonizing heartbreak as patients lost their battle. Our souls are forever scarred by the non-believers who heckled us, saying this was all just a hoax put on by the government. Hospitals were stretched for basic resources. The economy was wounded by massive layoffs. A country divided when it should have been united. Humanity seemed to be forgotten. Healthcare providers would never be the same. In the years that followed the pandemic, nurses fled from the bedside in tsunami-sized waves. Turnover remains constant in what seems to be a never-ending ripple effect.

Around May 5th, aunt Franca became ill with COVID-19. She was taken to the hospital, and Andy reached out for support. He, like everyone else, was not allowed to visit nor would he be allowed to go to the hospital. Franca died a few days later, no family with her because of restrictions. How sad and lonely for all those souls lost during that tragic time.

I have a picture of her wake. We were only allowed to have 10 guests. In the picture, Andy is sitting alone and Simi is by the casket. Such a pathetic scene. What an ugly time for our society. All of our norms were altered, all of our comfort was taken. We did rally together as a family at the cemetery. Even Rich was able to catch a flight to be there. A few weeks after Franca died, I received a call from Mom's memory care. The nurse asked me who Franca was. I filled her in on what had happened to Mom's sister. The nurse then told me that Mom was calling her name that day. I still get chills when I think about that phone call.

(May 14th, 2020. My cousin Andy sitting in the chair. Simi standing at the casket.)

On June 14th, the community started to open up just long enough for us to baptize our grandchild, Caroline. We were only allowed to have a few guests; we could not gather anywhere, but the heavens showed mercy and provided a beautiful day. We were able to bring both families together in the church parking lot. That afternoon, Jim and I went to see Mom. Visitation was only through a window. Mom was brought to the window in a wheelchair. She could barely stand. It had been a while since I laid eyes on Mom. I would call the nurses regularly to get status updates, but trying to talk to Mom over the phone ended months before. By now, she had lost over 40 pounds. Since quarantine, Dad was no longer able to visit in person, and as a result, Mom was no longer spoon fed as my dad would do. Sure, the staff would try to feed Mom, but there were a lot of residents and if Mom didn't show interest, she wouldn't be forced to eat. This was nature running its course. This was not cruelty. According to Mom's wishes, she was never to have a feeding tube. This was honored, and the price was weight loss. As difficult as this decision was, it was the correct one. But one that would hurt deeply and leave heavy guilt and perpetual doubt. I remember begging God for her death. She had suffered for too long.

By July 12th, the facility began allowing short outdoor visits that were by appointment only and at very limited times during the day. Dad and Simi were able to visit that week and as luck would have it, Mom was bright and able to speak a little. Dad even had her talk to another family member on the phone. I would later regret not getting to visit with Mom that week.

Also during July, as the world began to open up again, my family was facing big changes. Sonia moved to her first home on July 4th. Dad would move to his new condo on July 16th. Medicaid was approved, and we were granted entry for Mom to move to a facility within walking distance from our home. She would move in August, and Dad would be able to begin visiting again. Our condo, that was previously occupied by Sonia and her family, would close on August 14th, and Samantha would move out and close on her first home in September. We couldn't help but feel like things were falling into place. Mom would be in her old neighborhood, and Dad no longer had to drive 30 minutes to visit her. Financial worries were under control. The first wave of COVID-19 relaxed, so we could all feel some remnant of normalcy.

The last breath

On July 18th, two short days after Dad moved to his condo, I got the call from the nurse. She let me know Mom took a turn for the worse and fell unresponsive. Dad and I drove out to see her. Jim would drive Simi just a few minutes behind us. As fate would have it, Rich was in Indiana visiting his in-laws and was planning to come see Dad's new condo the following week, so it only took him a few hours to get to Mom.

Mom was a skeleton of her former self. She was unresponsive, breathing shallow with her mouth open. It took Dad some time to figure out how to talk to her. So sad to watch him grieve. Deep down, I knew Dad would be able to move on. I thought to myself that it was another blessing that Mom would die first. Mom's depression would not have allowed her to recover if Dad were to have passed away first. I also reflected on the end of this nightmare and that Mom's suffering was finally going to end.

Rich arrived around midnight, and I went home to be with my family. He and Dad went home for some rest and a shower in the early morning hours. Simi and I returned to Mom's side around 8 am. Mom was hanging on, but the end was near. Hospice had been with Mom all night, ensuring her breathing remained comfortable. It was around 10 am when Mom took her last breath. I felt this strong need to read something to Mom so I found a blessing that I quietly recited to her. And then just like that, my mother was gone. I said goodbye to an extraordinary woman who was so genuine and caring. Someone who could never be replaced.

Recovery

Dad would break down frequently as expected and then began to recover. I did most of my grieving upfront. I mourned every loss, every stage because I knew how this would end. Dad, on the other hand, was overwhelmed with the process itself and consumed with trying to keep Mom oriented. He blamed himself for Mom's weight loss and her shutting down mentally. No amount of reassurance or explanation of the disease course would get through. It was just his way of processing. Dad was fortunate that we were allowed many guests for Mom's funeral. All of whom brought a piece of Mom with them in the form of a story or memory. It was like Mom was whole again. Many reflected on the anniversary party just a few short years earlier and thanked us for bringing the family together to celebrate Mom and Dad when they both could enjoy it. Some even donned their scarves. I was not ready to deal with so many guests, but Dad needed his community around him.

After about a year, Dad started to show signs of healing. His social structure was restored with COVID-19 restrictions lifted. My niece, Mary Angela, spent the summer with him before she would marry in the fall. Dad, Caroline, and I went to visit Mom's grave on what would have been her 84th birthday. I was chasing after Caroline when I turned back and saw Dad. He was leaning on the wall facing Mom's final resting place, the pain still evident, the love still felt and the depth of grief eternal.

(July 8th, 2021)

Epilogue/Conclusion

On July 22nd, 2020, Rich and I took care of mom's belongings at her memory care facility and wrote the following email to their director.

> *We will be picking up Nara's belongings today, officially saying goodbye. We cannot express how deeply our family has appreciated the love, support, and care shown to Nara and Aldo. I'm sure you understand that it is never an easy decision to place a loved one in memory care. I personally felt as though I gave up on Mom and that was tied to so many emotions. Your staff immediately embraced Nara as family and learned what she would best respond to so that she would trust and feel safe. Even on difficult days, staff maintained the highest level of professionalism. They are all a gift. Everyone from you, the nurses, the aids, the activity directors, housekeepers, the handyman, and kitchen staff, welcomed us and looked out for Nara.*
>
> *Thank you is woefully inadequate.*
>
> *Please tell staff that they will always be remembered as the wonderful family that helped Mom live up until her darkest hours and in her darkest hours, they loved.*

I'm not one to go to cemeteries; in fact, I made my family swear never to place my body in one. The orders they have are to cremate me at the lowest cost possible and spread my ashes wherever they desire. I grieve in private and would rather be in my head than staring at a cold and overpriced headstone. I certainly do not want anyone to feel an obligation to visit a cemetery either. Regardless, I wanted something to remind me of mom and found myself thinking about a tattoo of all things. It was an idea that crept up during Mom's final stages. Understand that I have never gotten a tattoo. For some reason, it felt right so I got to designing. I had seen the image of a dandelion with the seeds flying away which made me think of the impact of Alzheimer's on the brain, slowly stealing parts from the whole. It has been a symbol for the disease, so not terribly original of me. The stem was the scripted phrase "forget me not" that leads to the head of the flower. On January 8th, 2021, the design became a permanent part of me. A very good friend of mine came with to offer support, and I was grateful for the company. In closing, here are a few words of advice. What I learned through this journey and hope to have instilled is to allow yourself grace. Whether you have a family member with Alzheimer's or cancer or terminal whatever, give yourself grace as you process. If you feel as though you made a mistake, give yourself grace. No one has gone through what you are going through in the exact same way. There is no right or wrong, only what *feels* right and wrong. Keep the pieces together for as long as you can, but learn to let go with grace when the time comes.

Acknowledgments

How do I begin?

This memoir detailed the difficulties I perceived my father was having as he tried to be the main caregiver for Mom. When it comes down to it, he deserves all the credit for keeping Mom out of memory care for as long as we did. Aldo Giuntini is as strong as they come. He kept his vows and cared for Mom for better *and* worse. Thank you, Dad, you are an inspiration to all of us.

To my husband Jim and my aunt Simi, there are no words that would adequately express my gratitude for both of you. The countless phone calls, last-minute interventions, the search party, the shoulder to cry on, and the ear to scream in.

To Rich and Theresa, thank you for always being there, for answering my phone calls and listening to the stories, and for your undying support.

To the grandkids, for always showing your love even when Nonna was no longer acting like herself. This must have been so hard and confusing to watch, yet none of you shied away.

To my dear friend Coleen, who would drop everything just to pour me a glass of wine.

To my extended family and friends, we always felt your support, love and kindness.

To my work family, for understanding whenever I had to leave unexpectedly, make last minute schedule changes, or had a short fuse.

Thank you all

Printed in the United States
by Baker & Taylor Publisher Services